THIS COLORING BOOK

BELONGS TO:

____

____

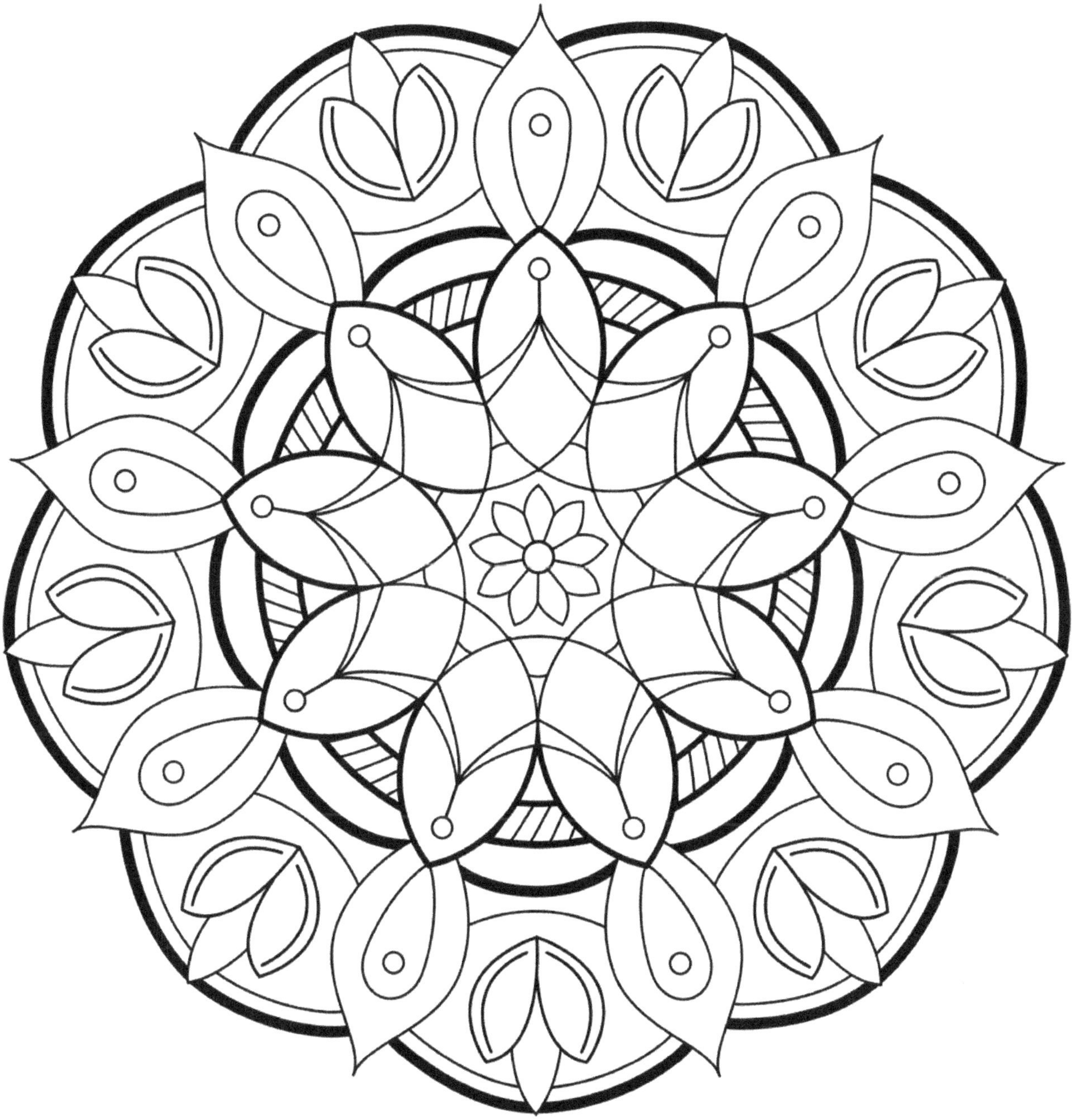

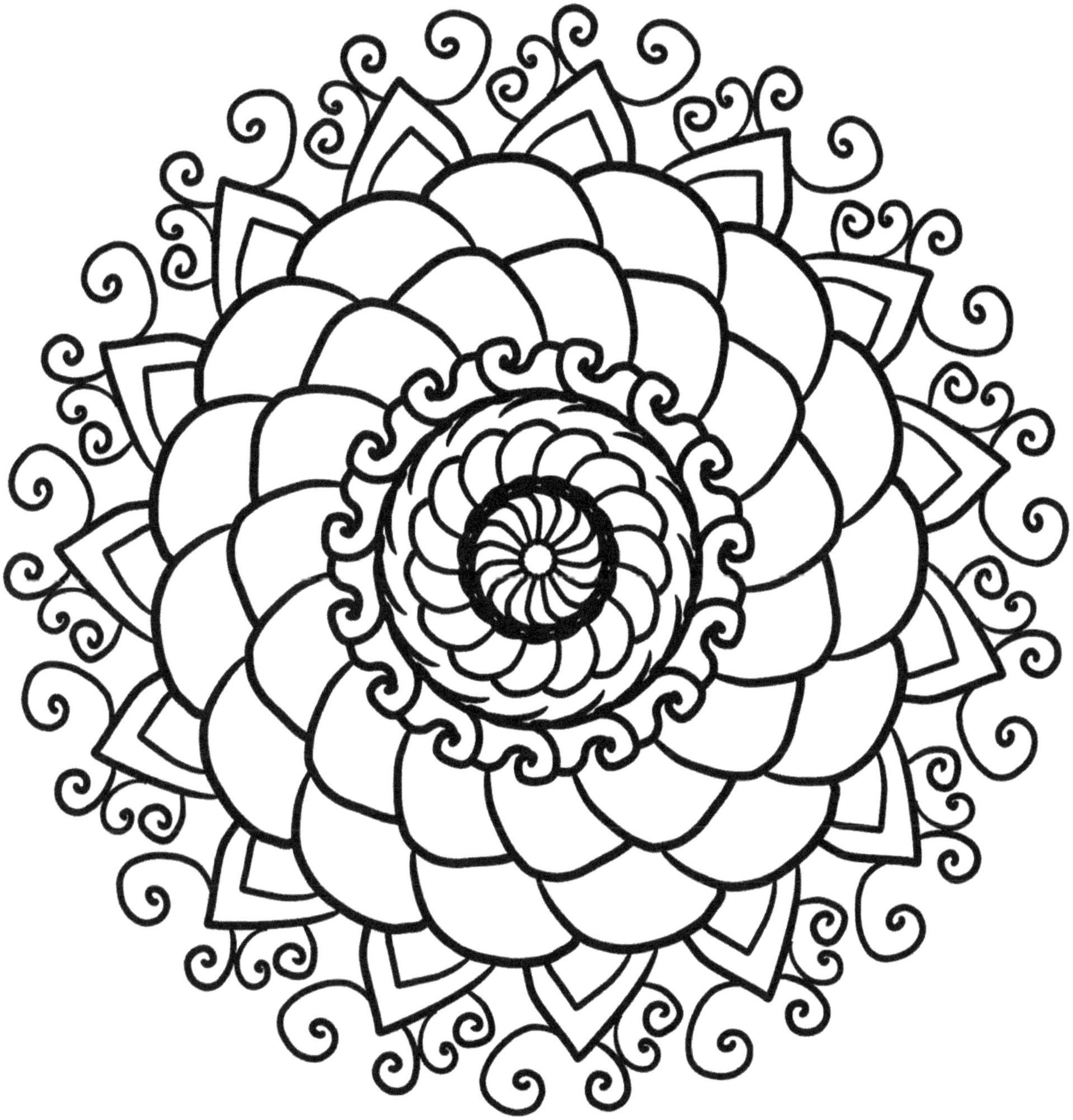

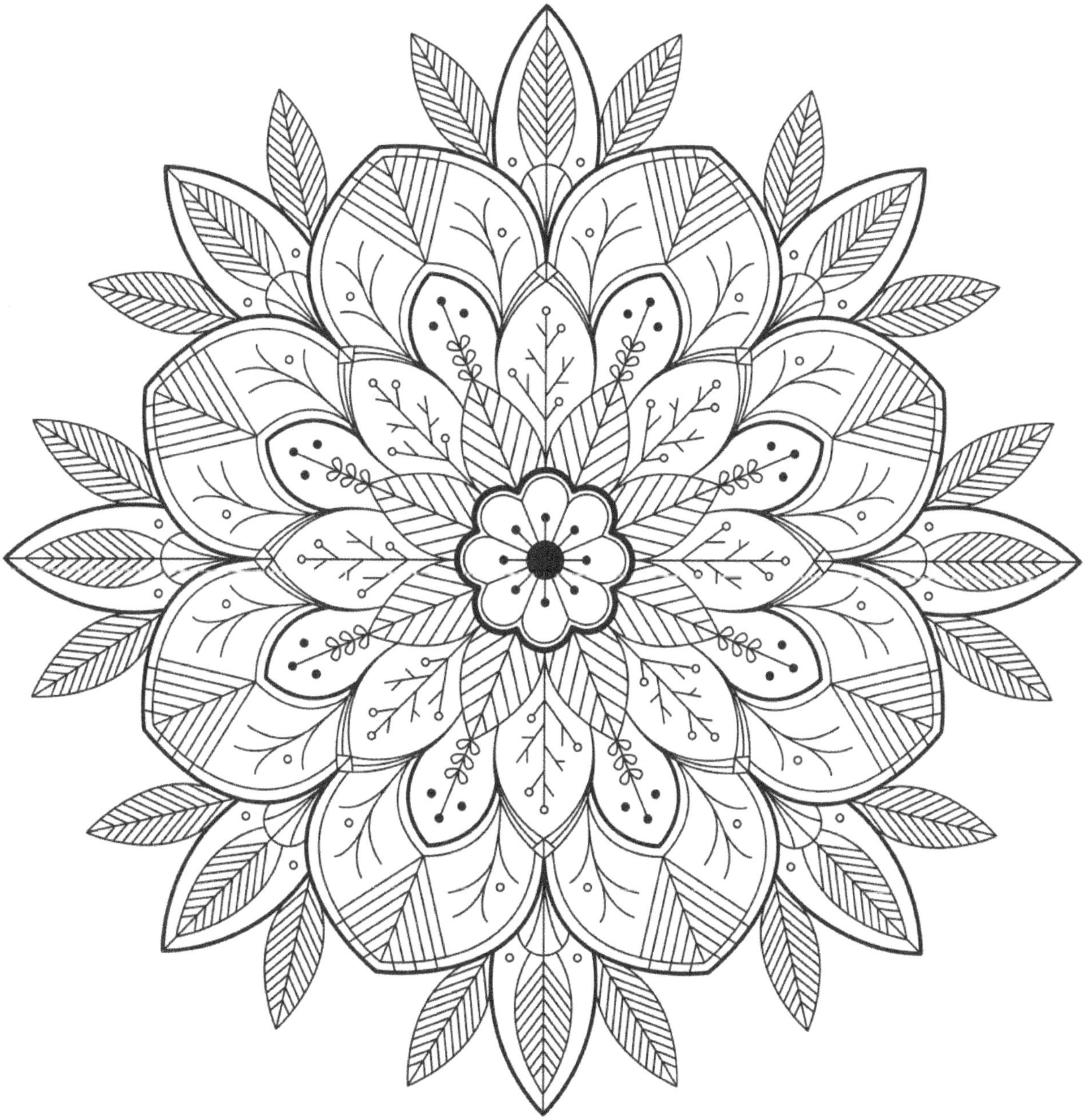

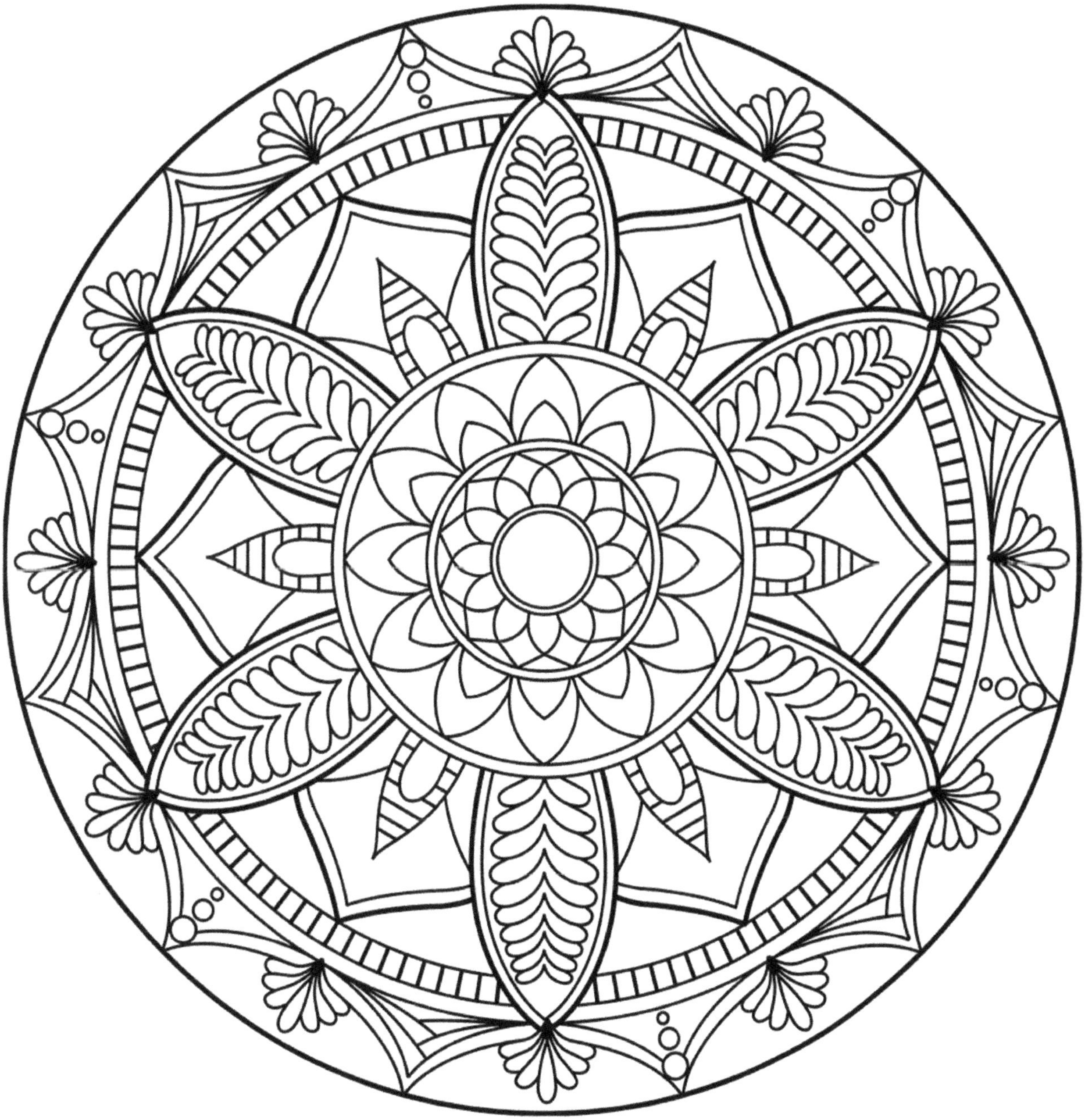

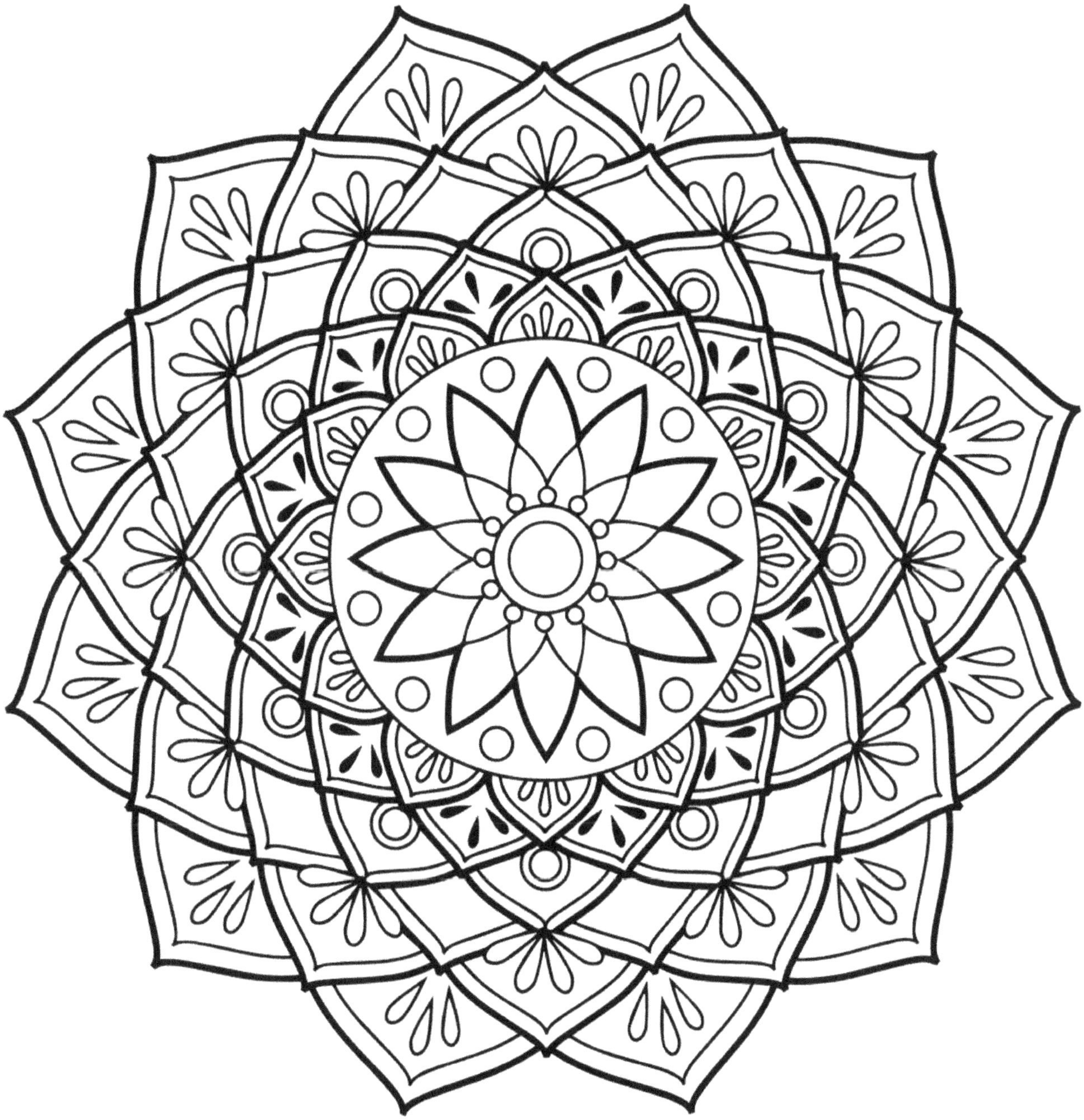

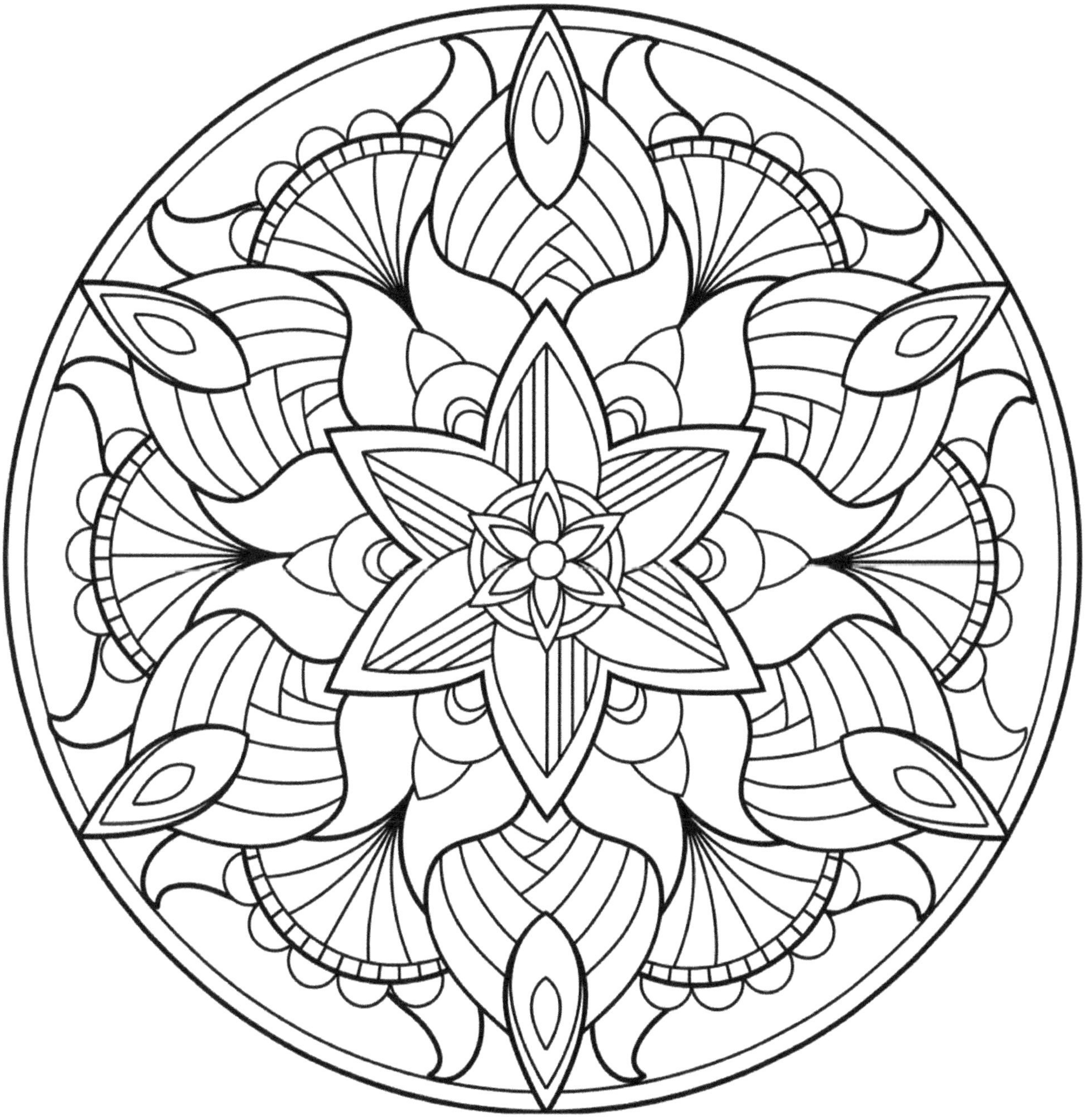

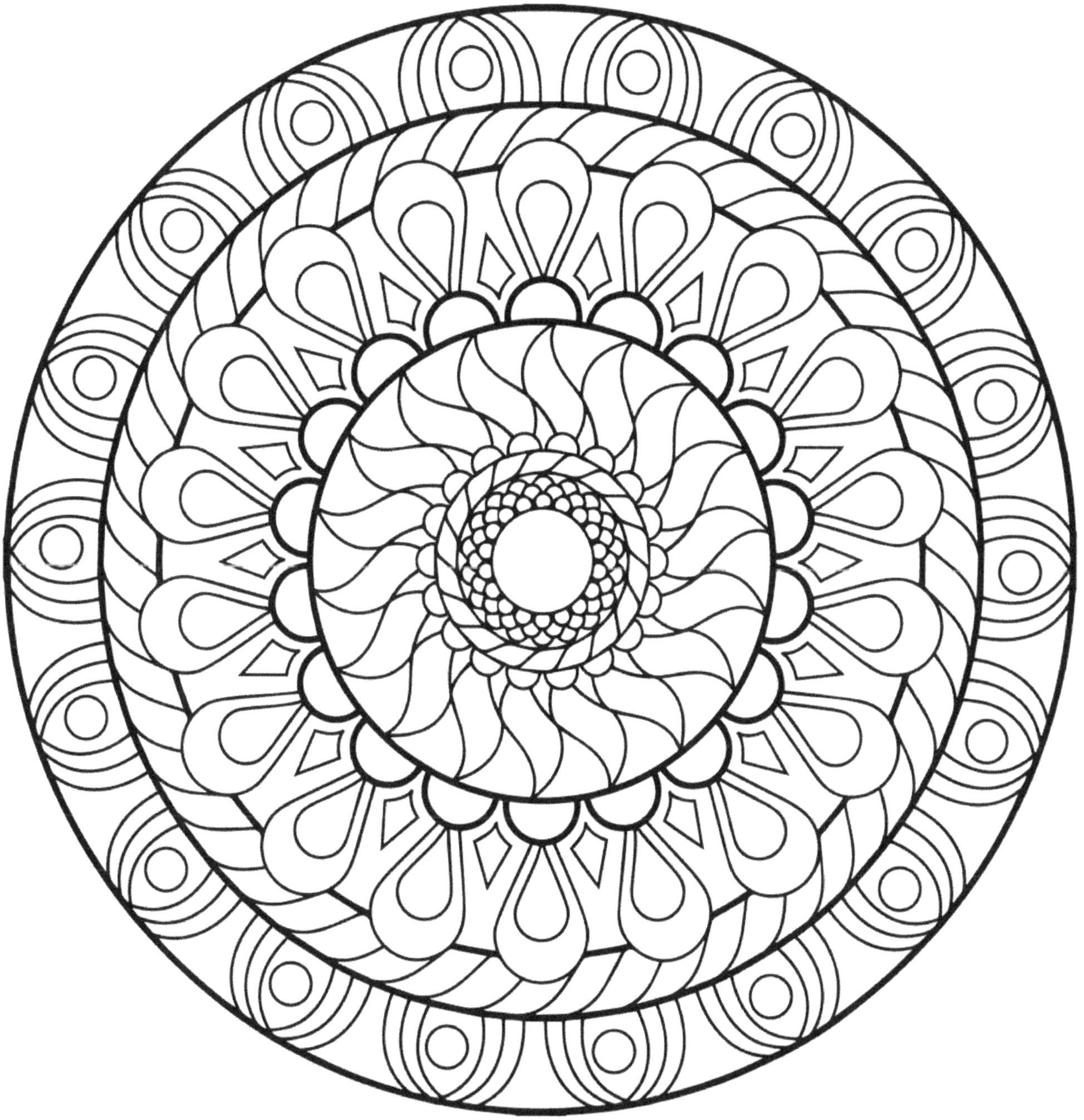

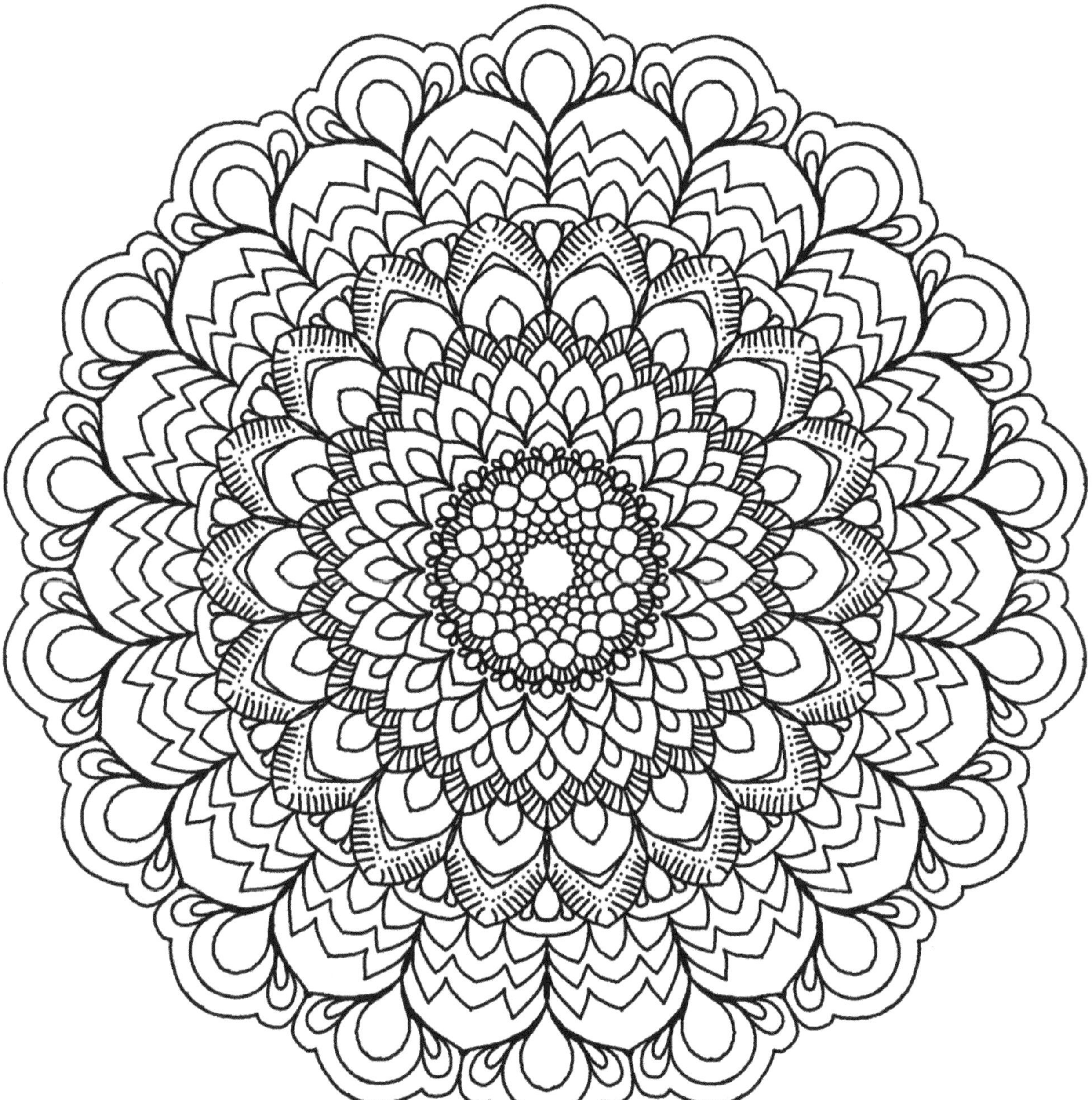

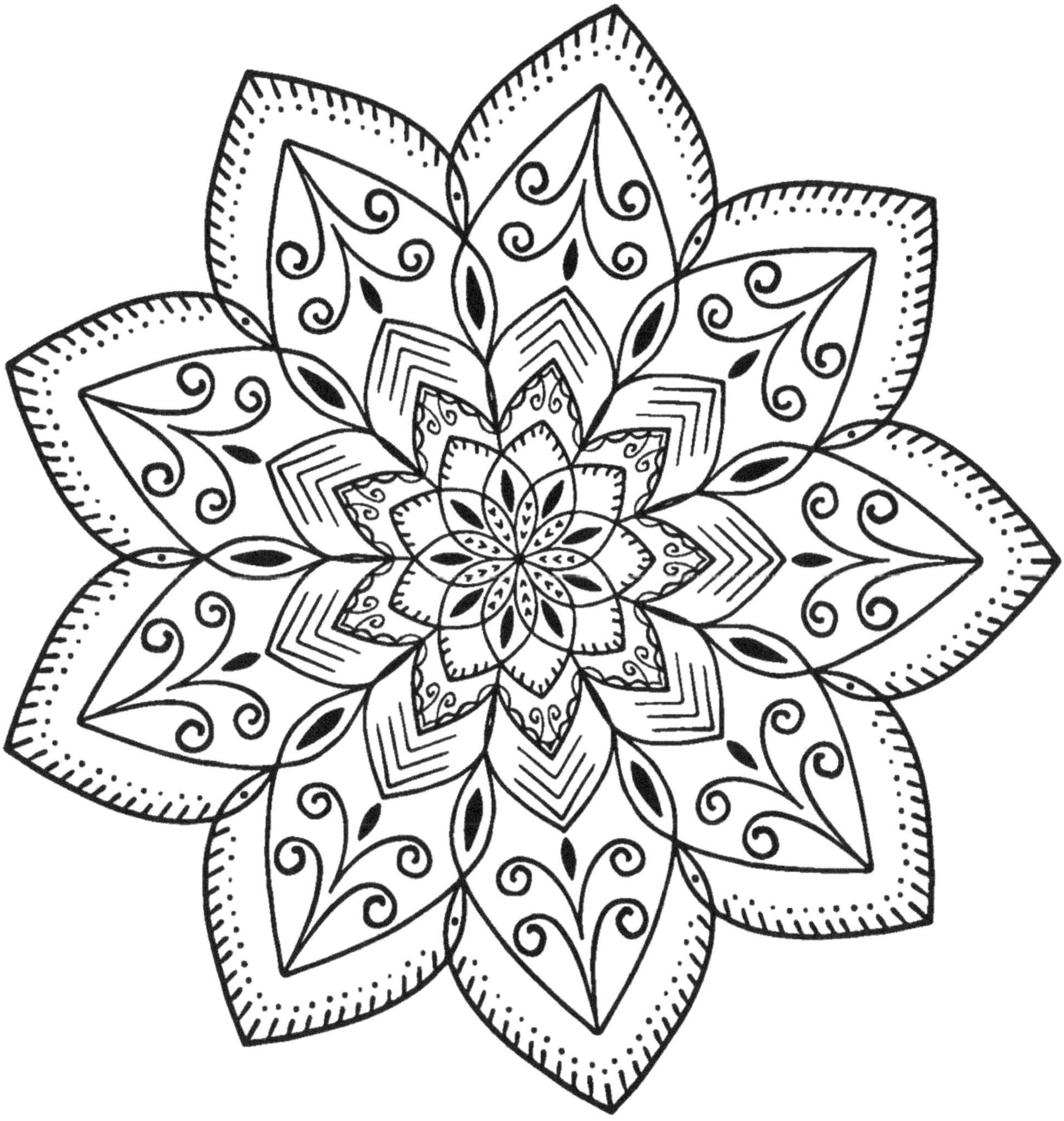

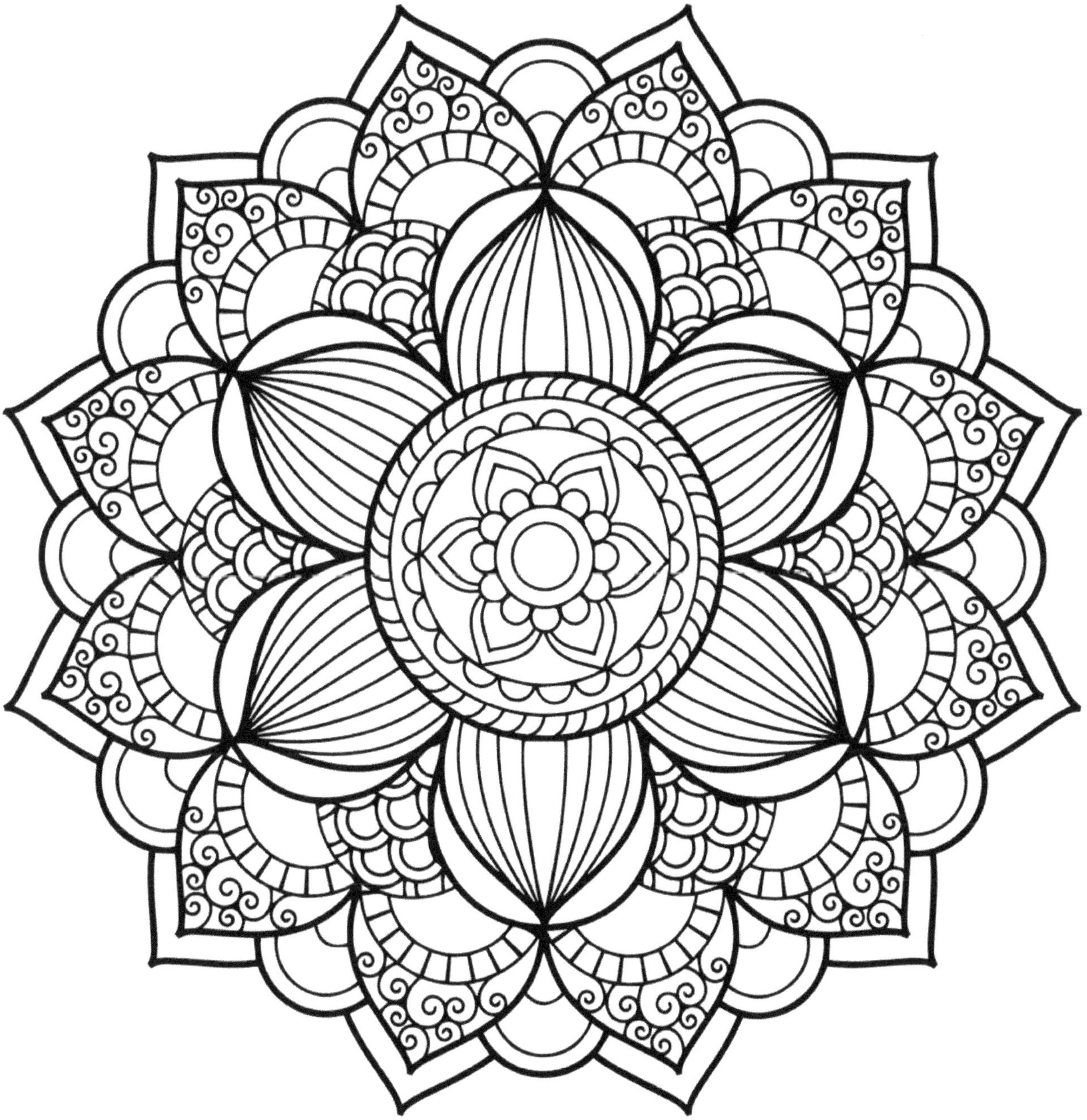

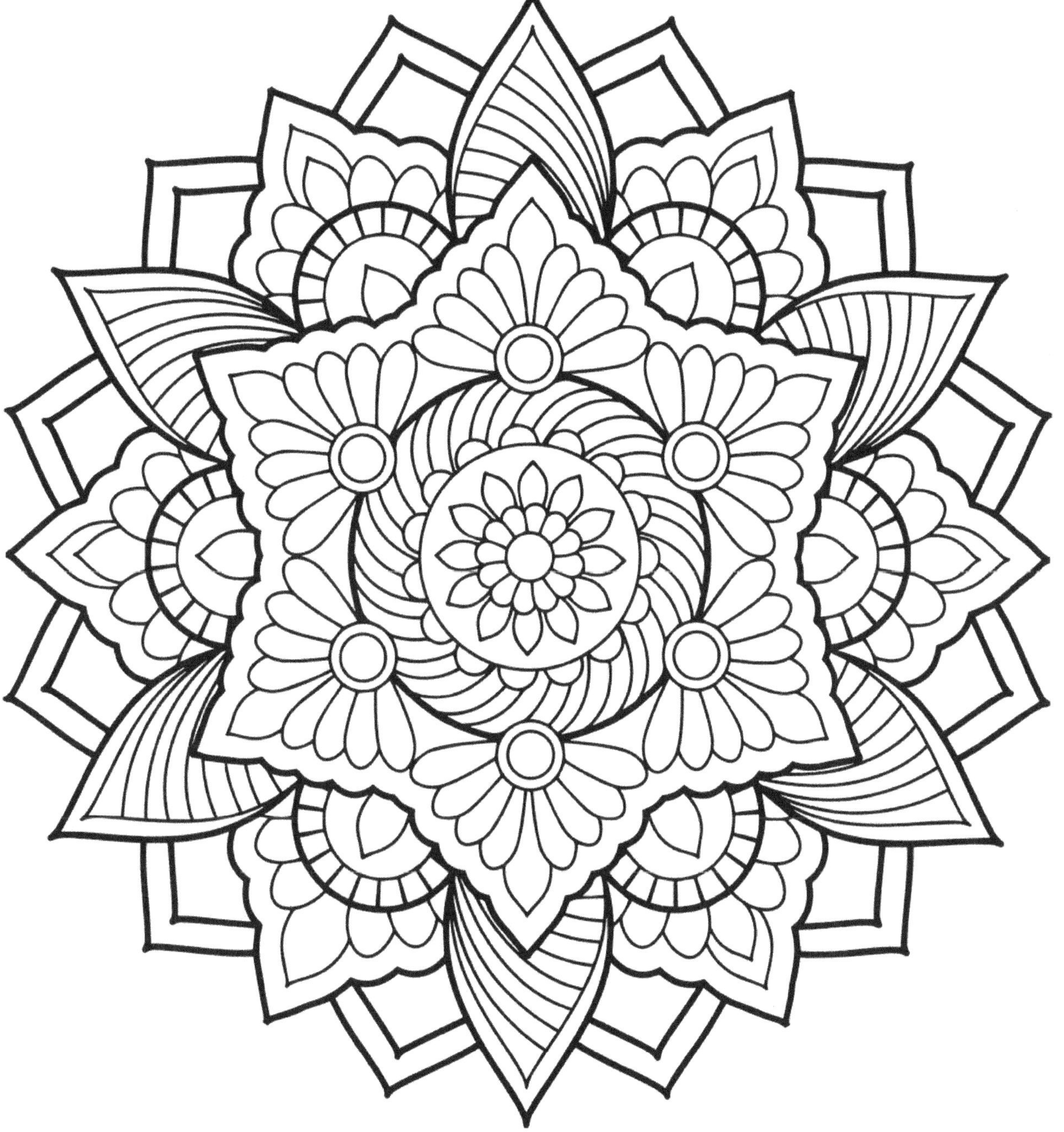

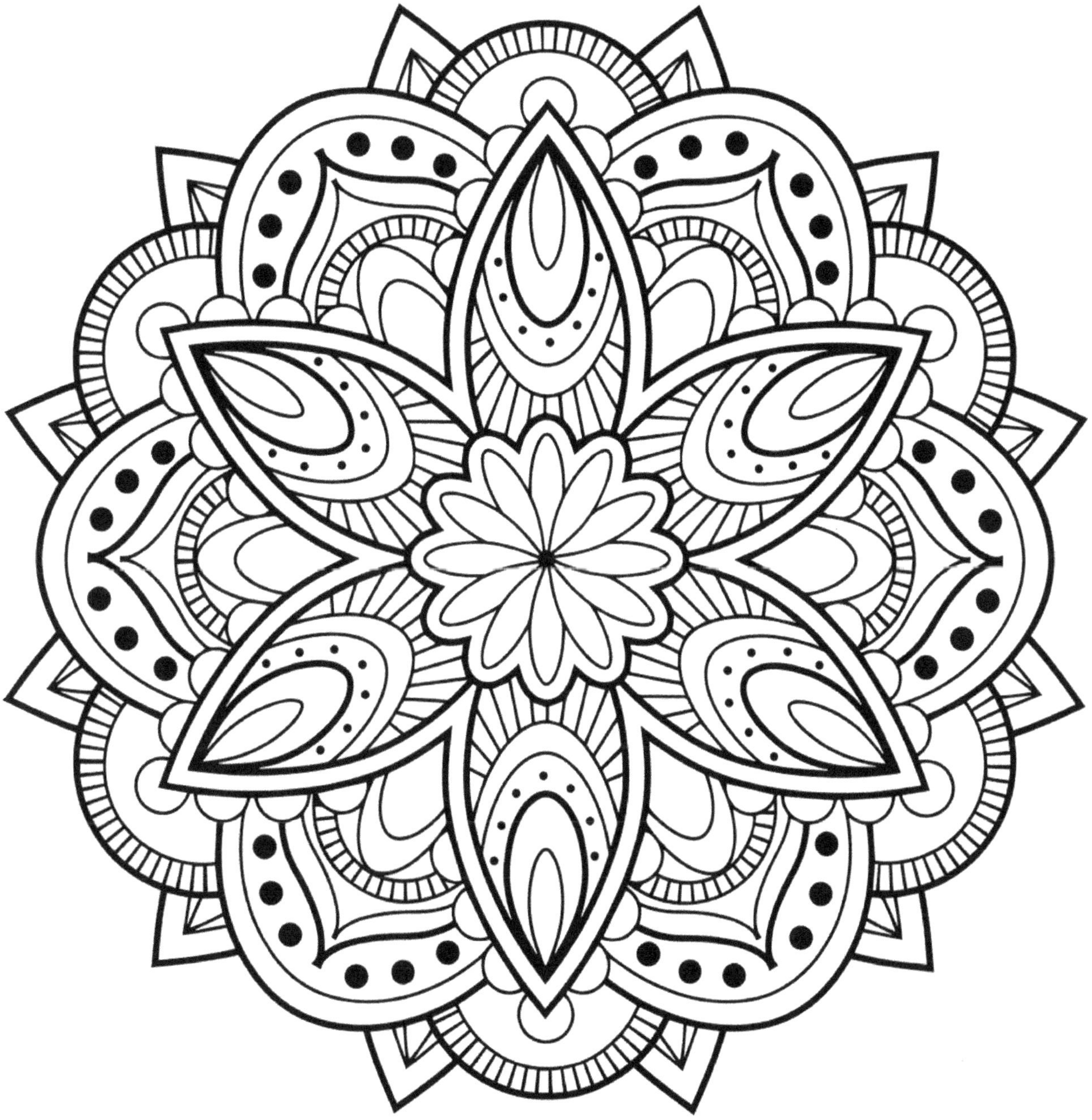

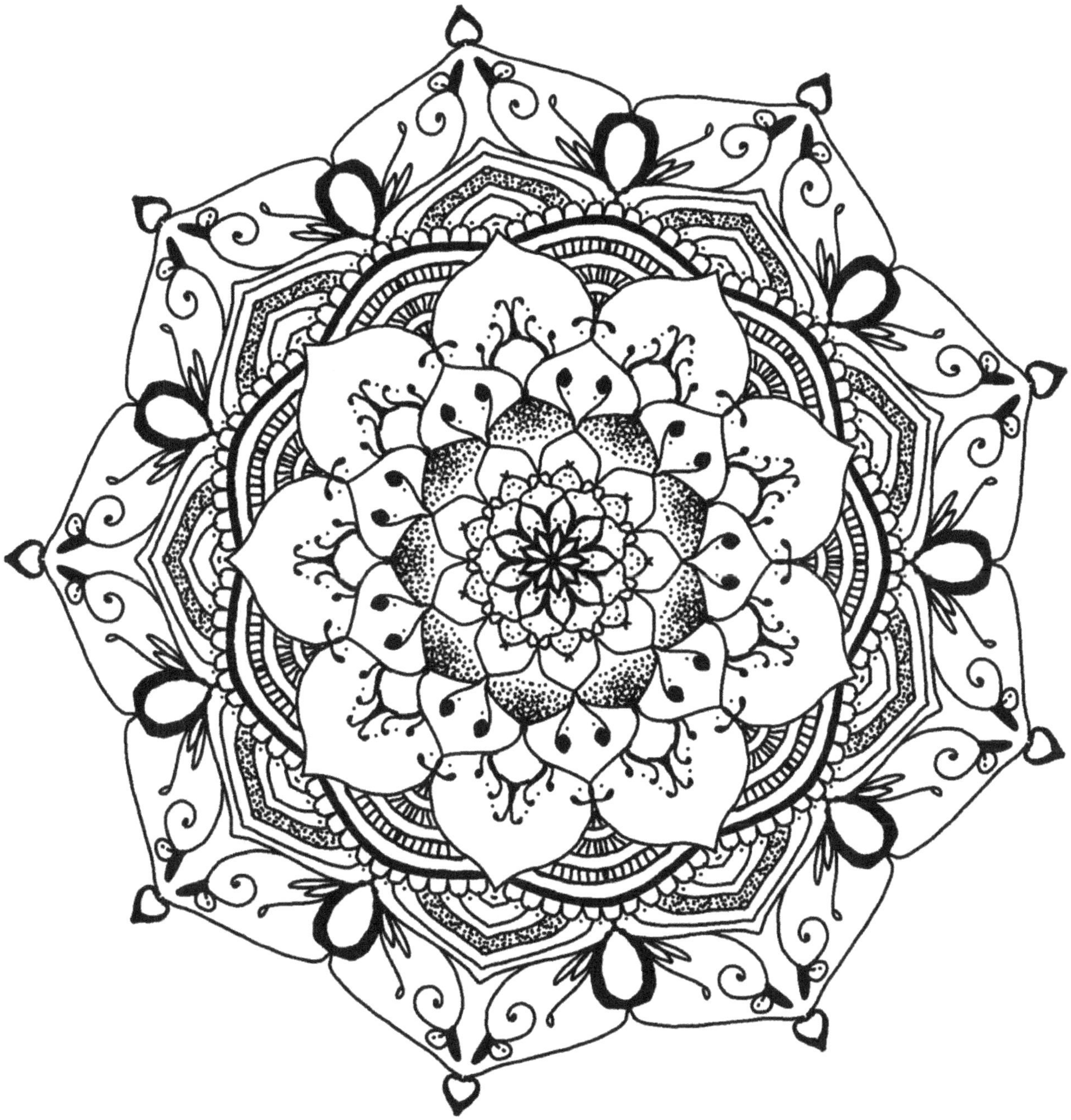

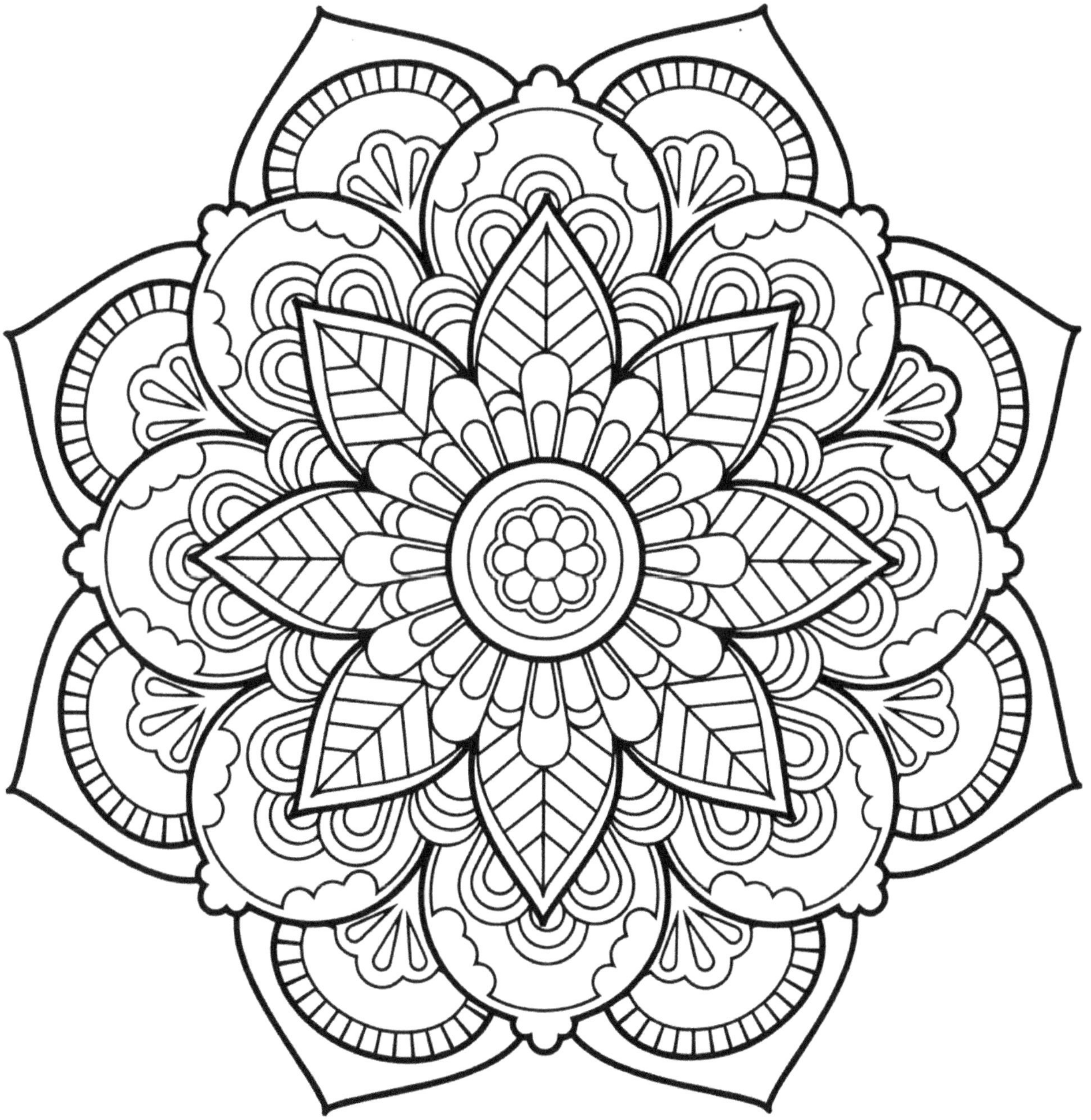

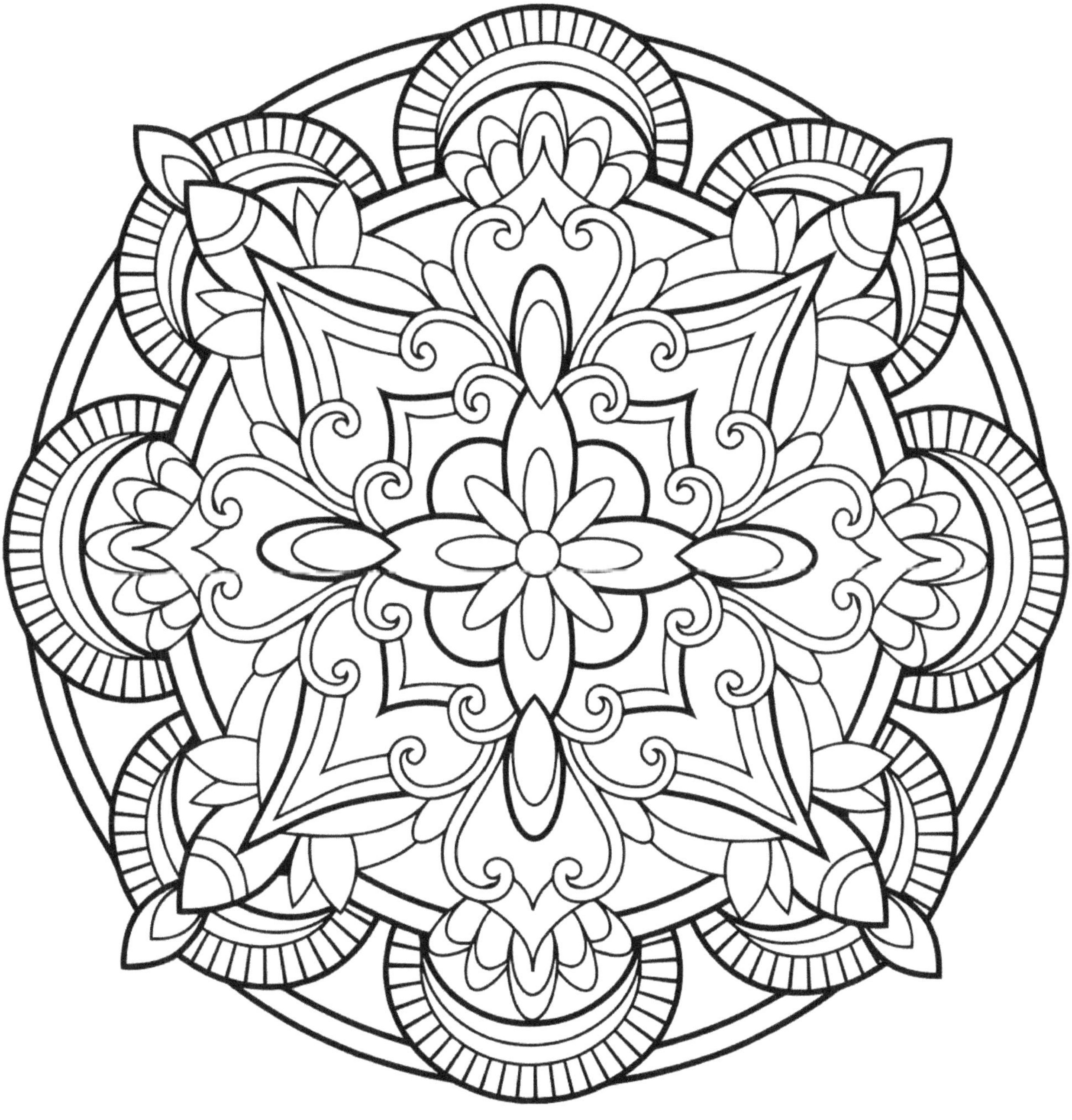

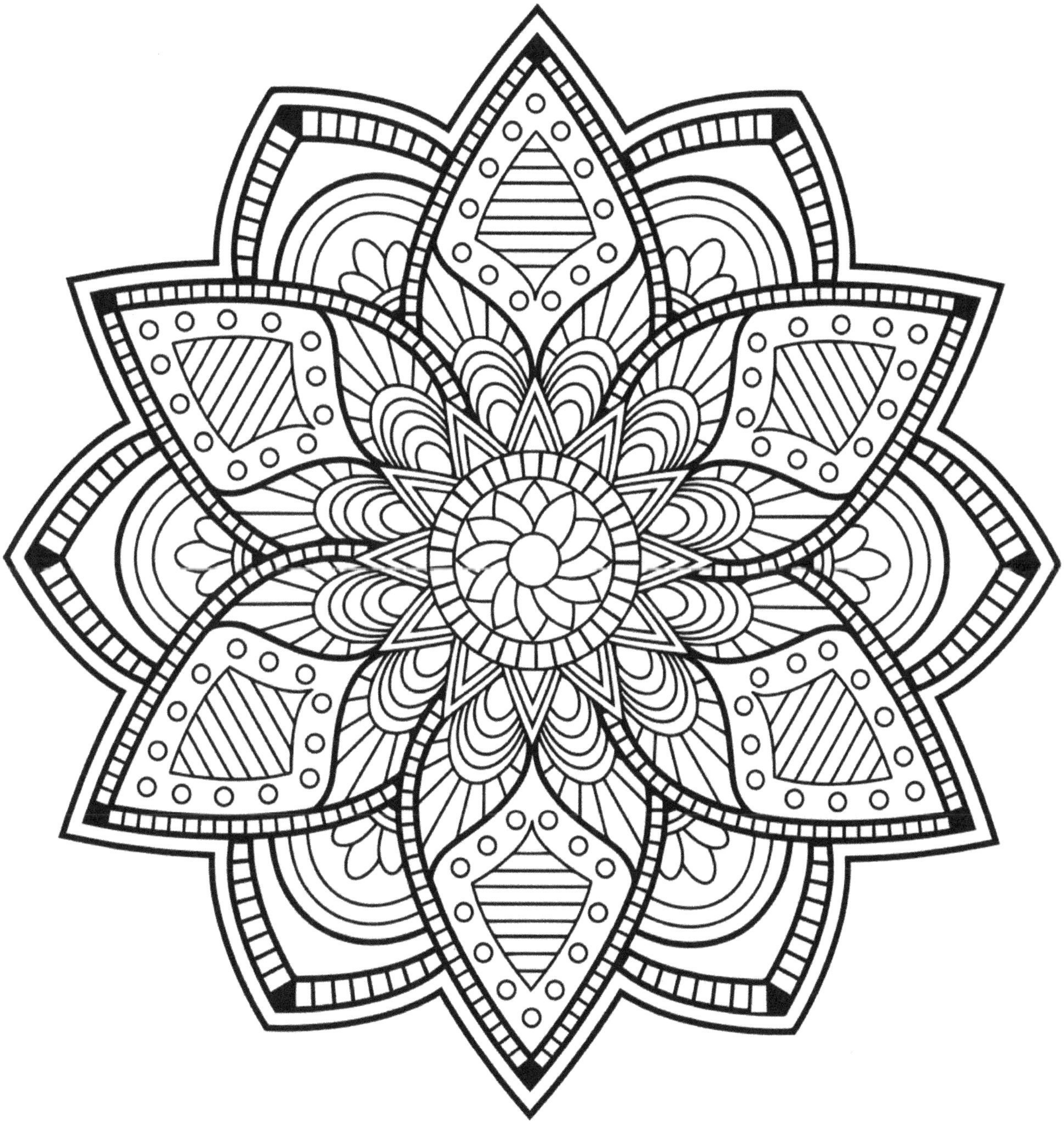

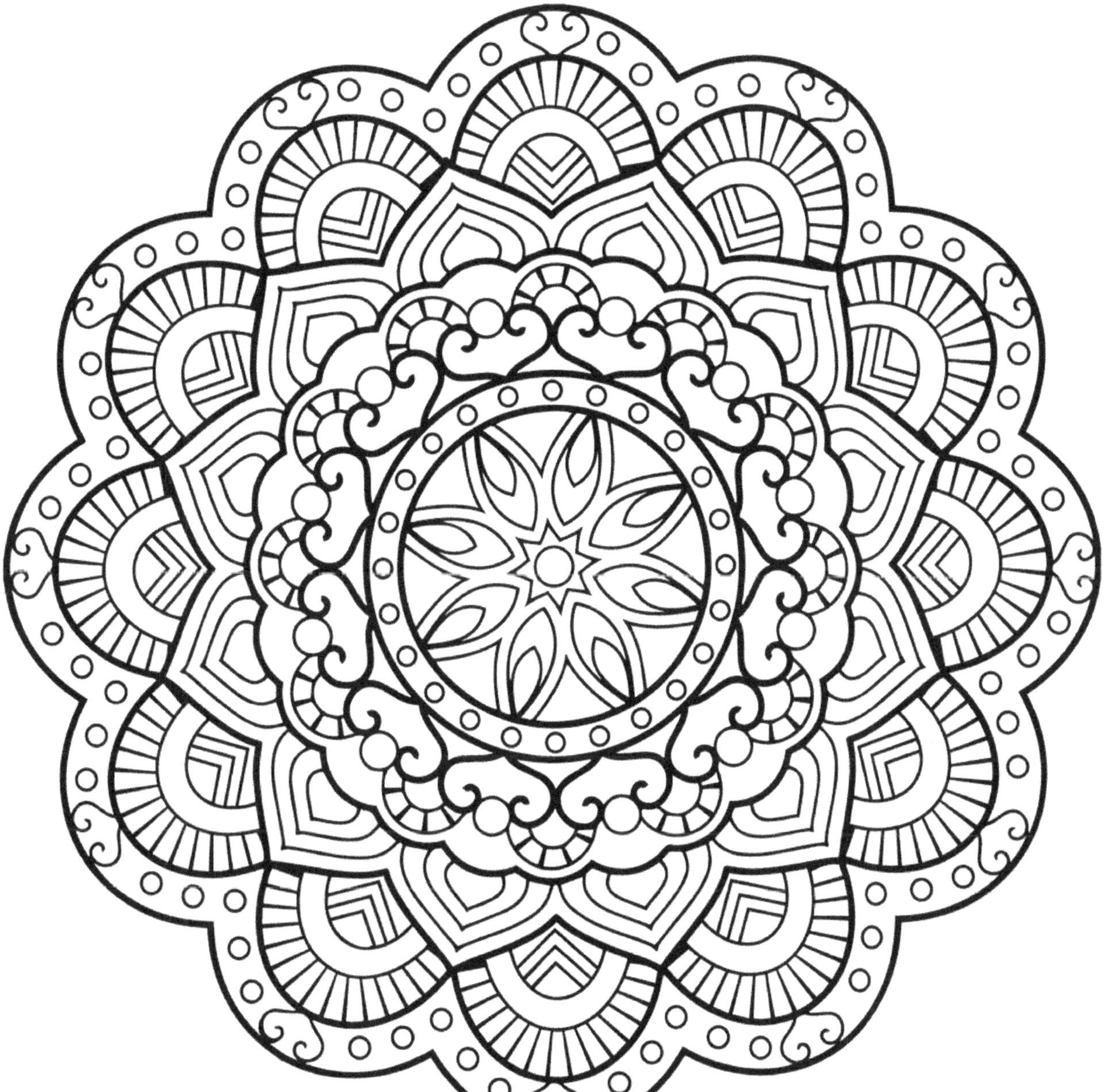

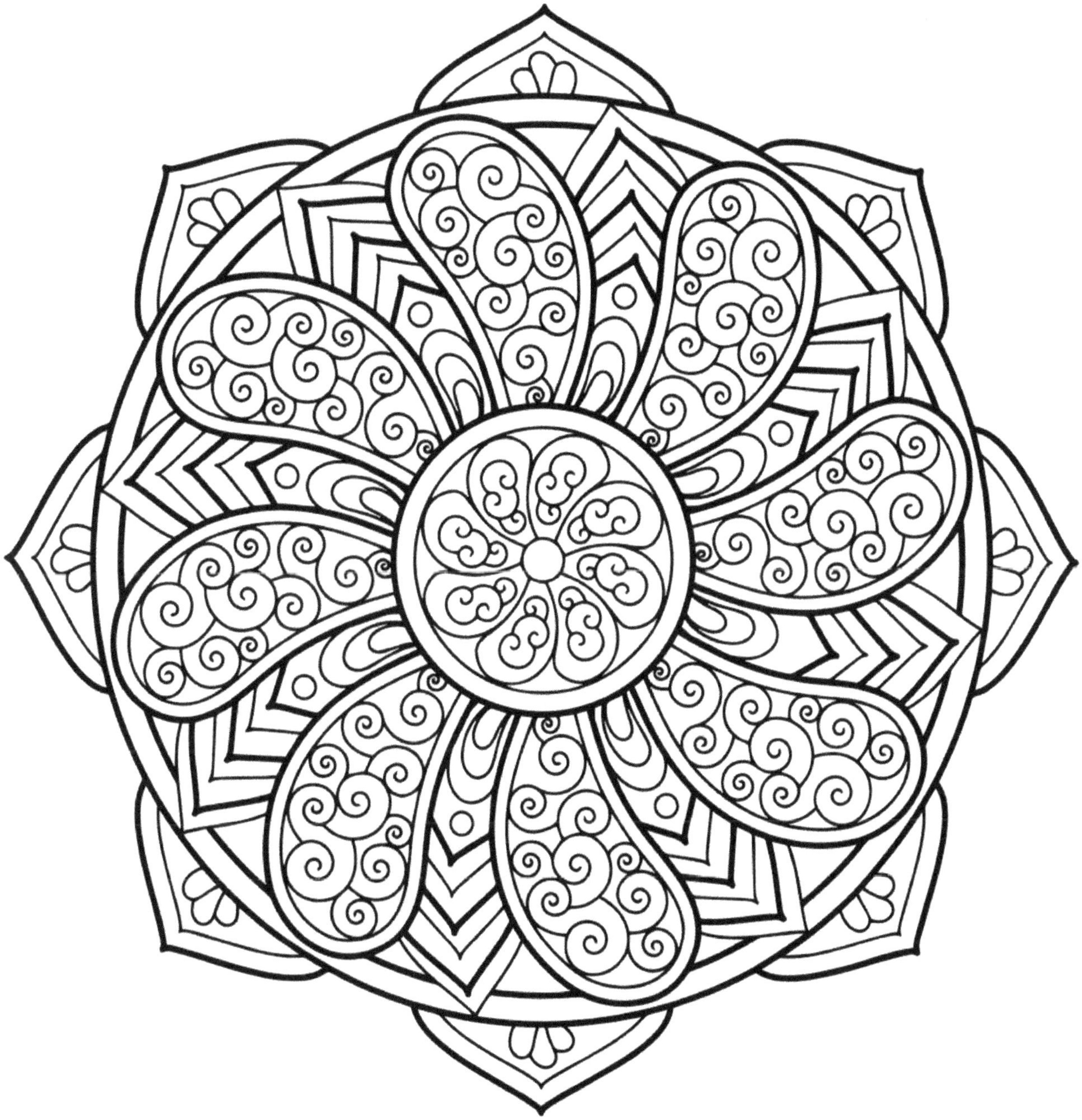

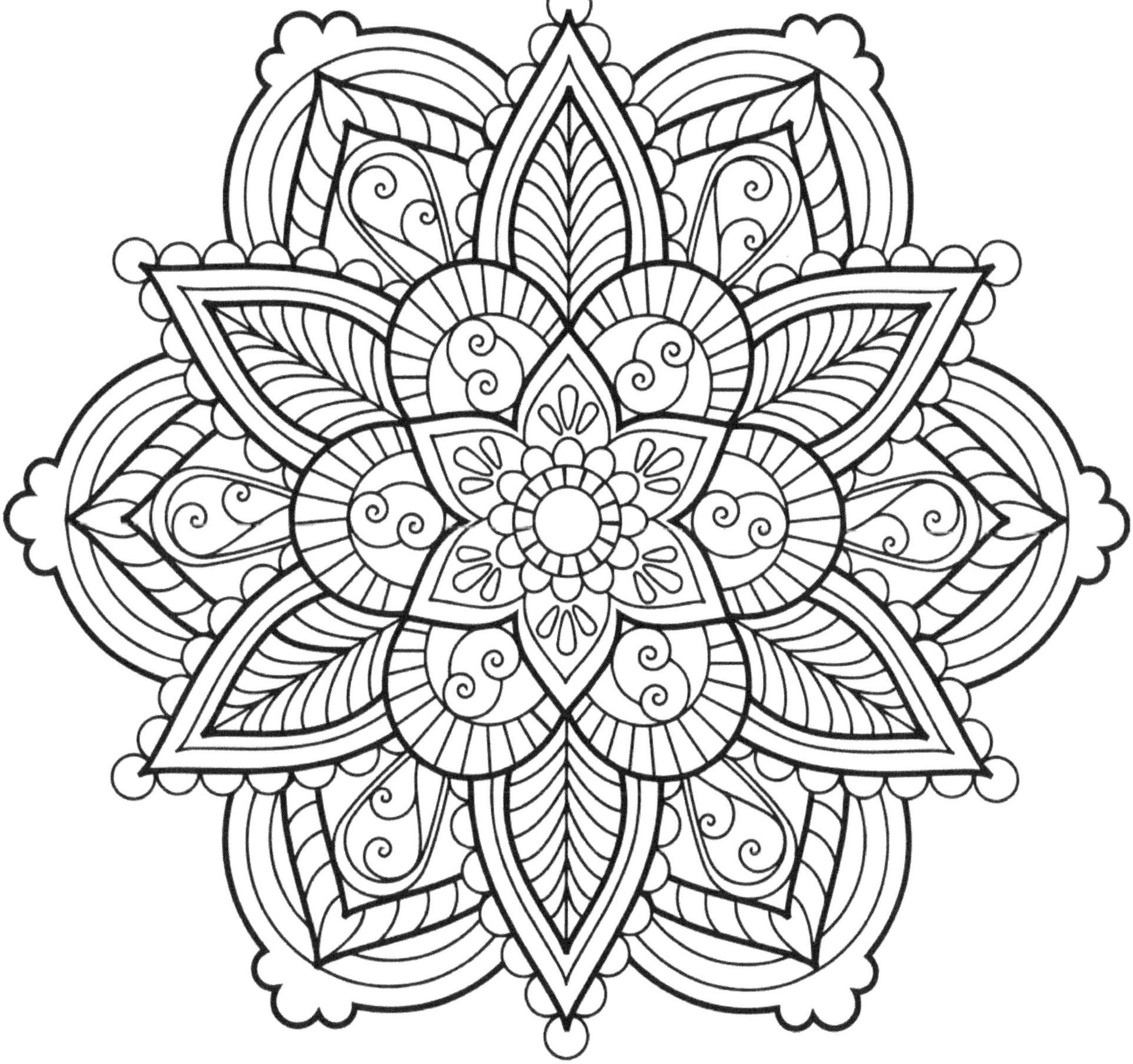

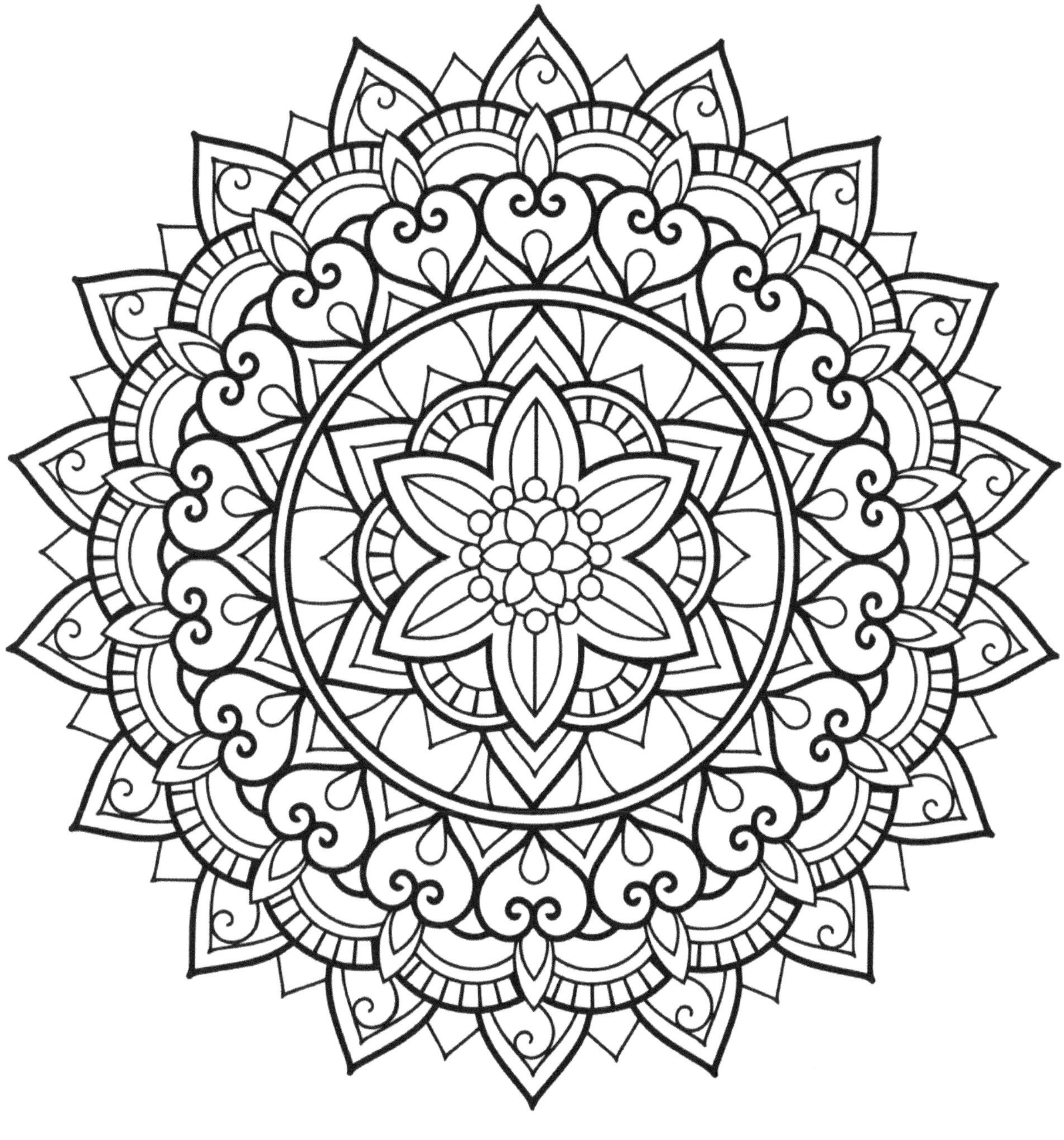

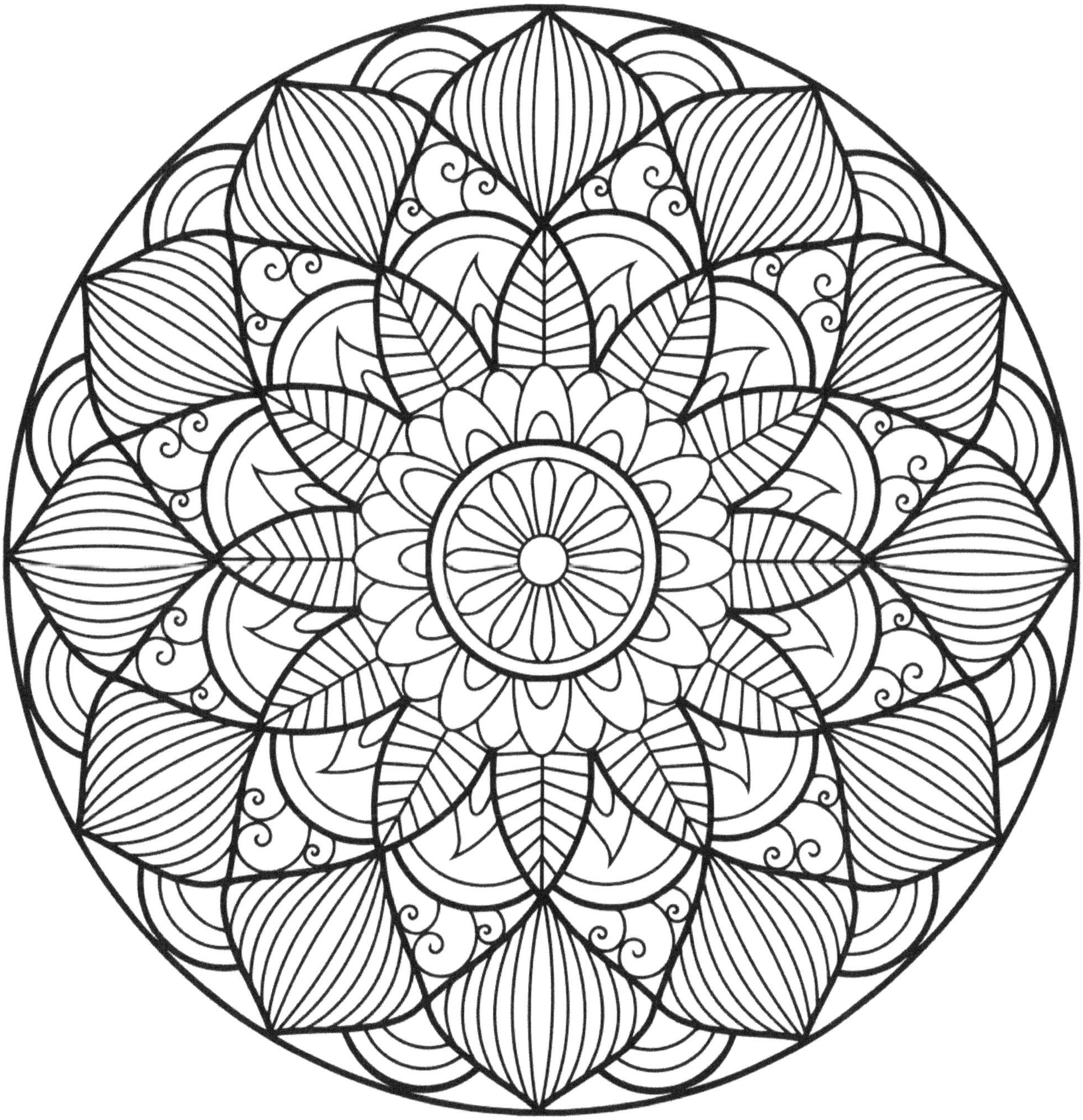

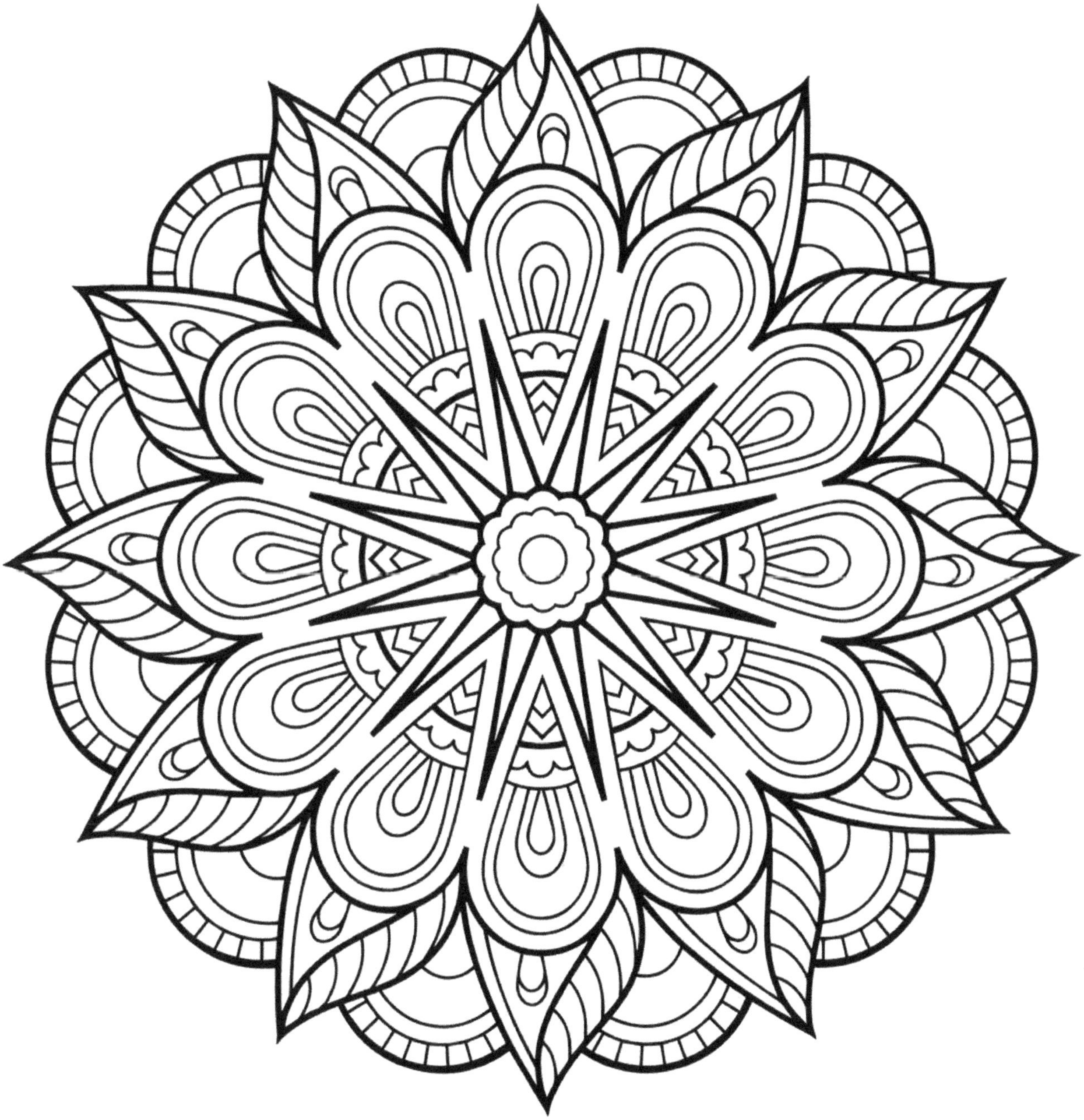

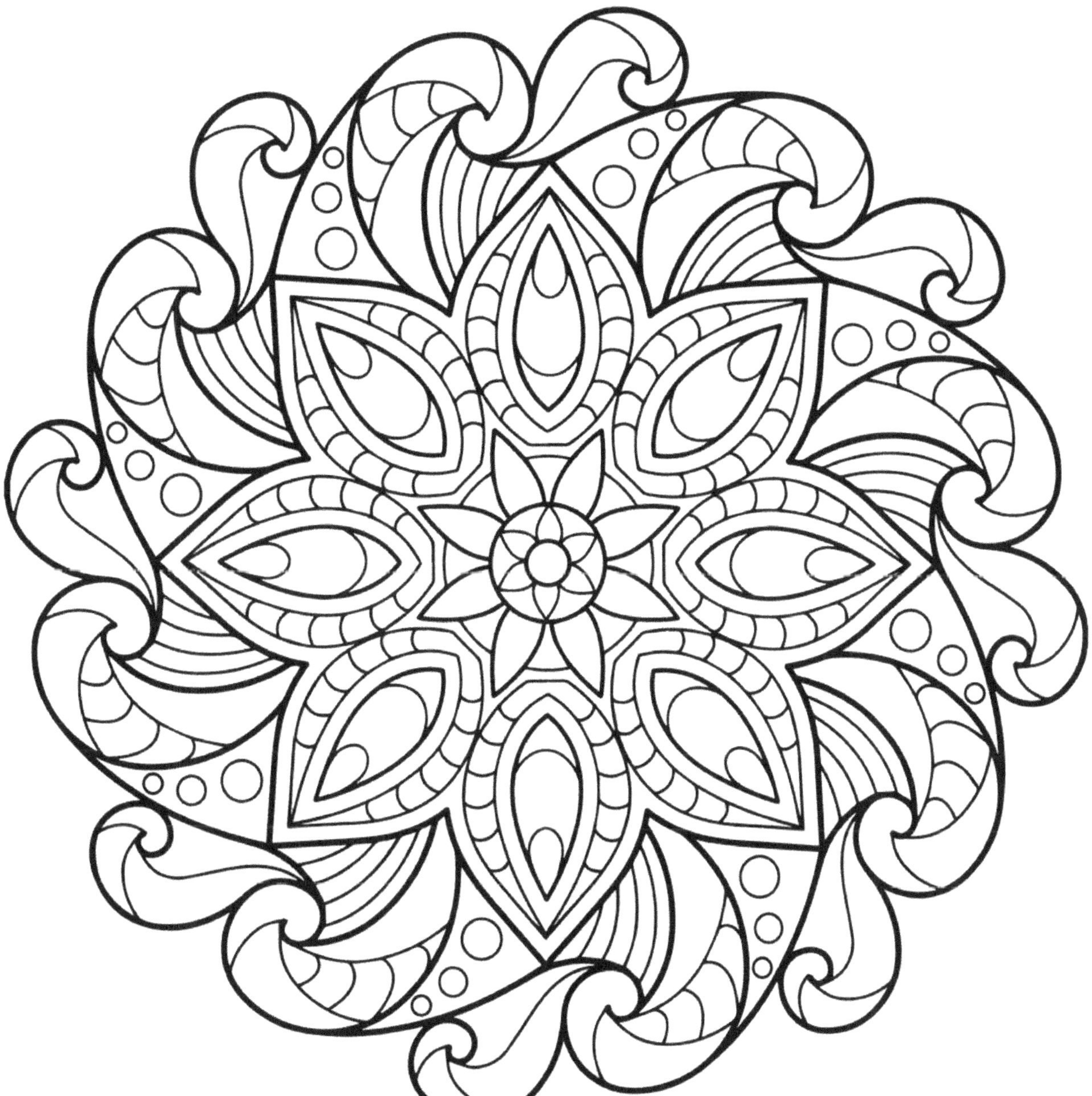

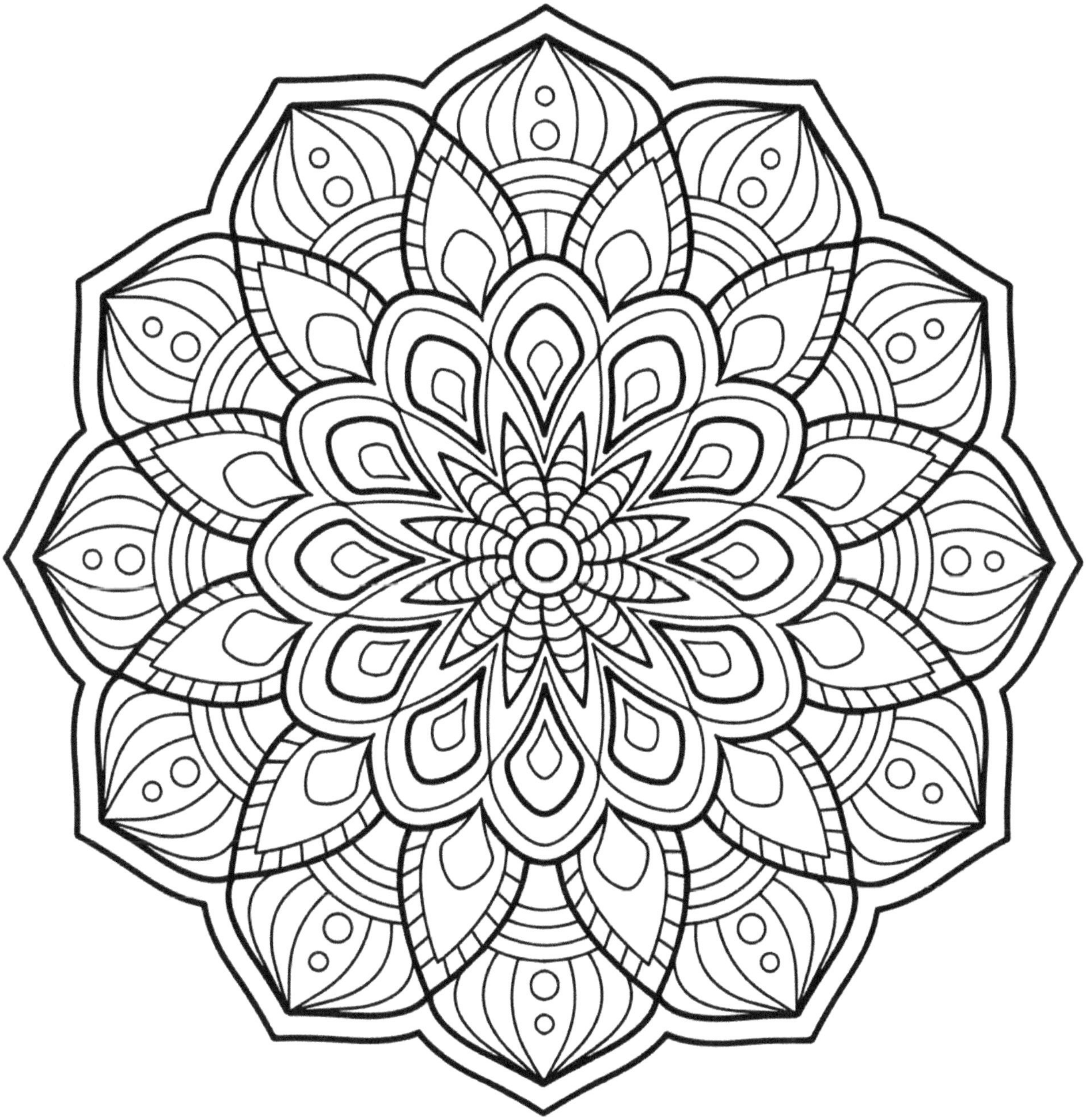

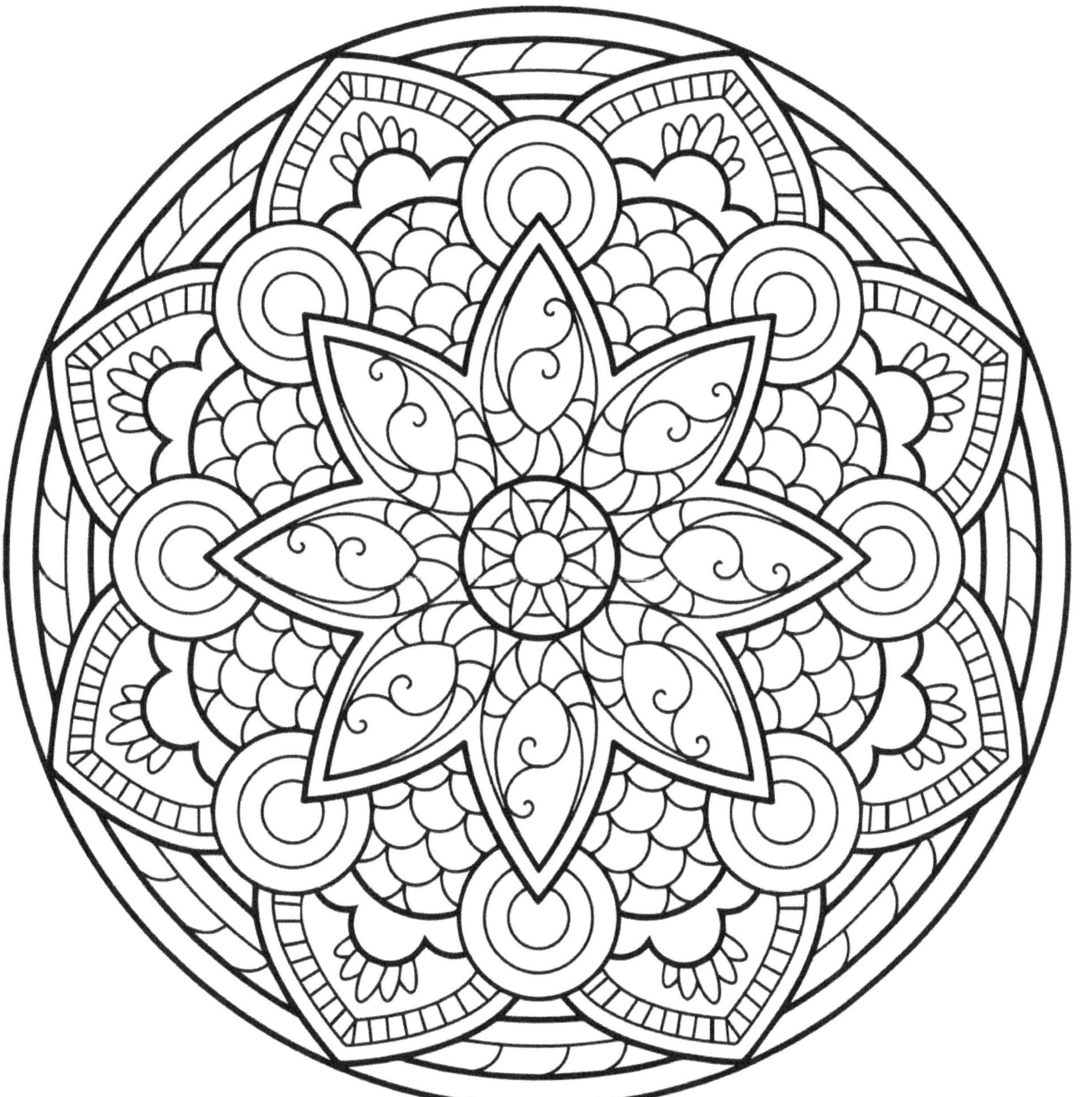

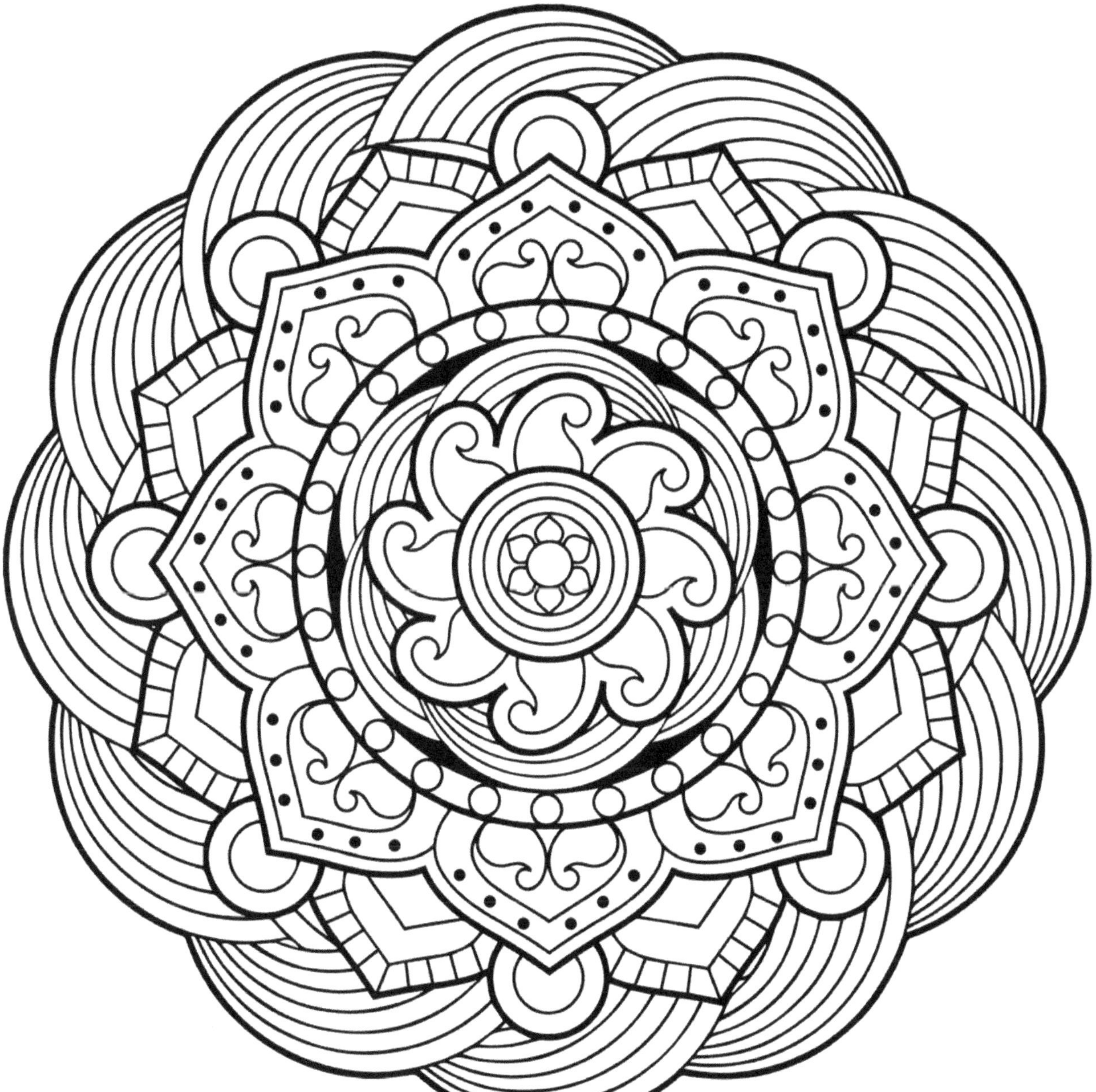

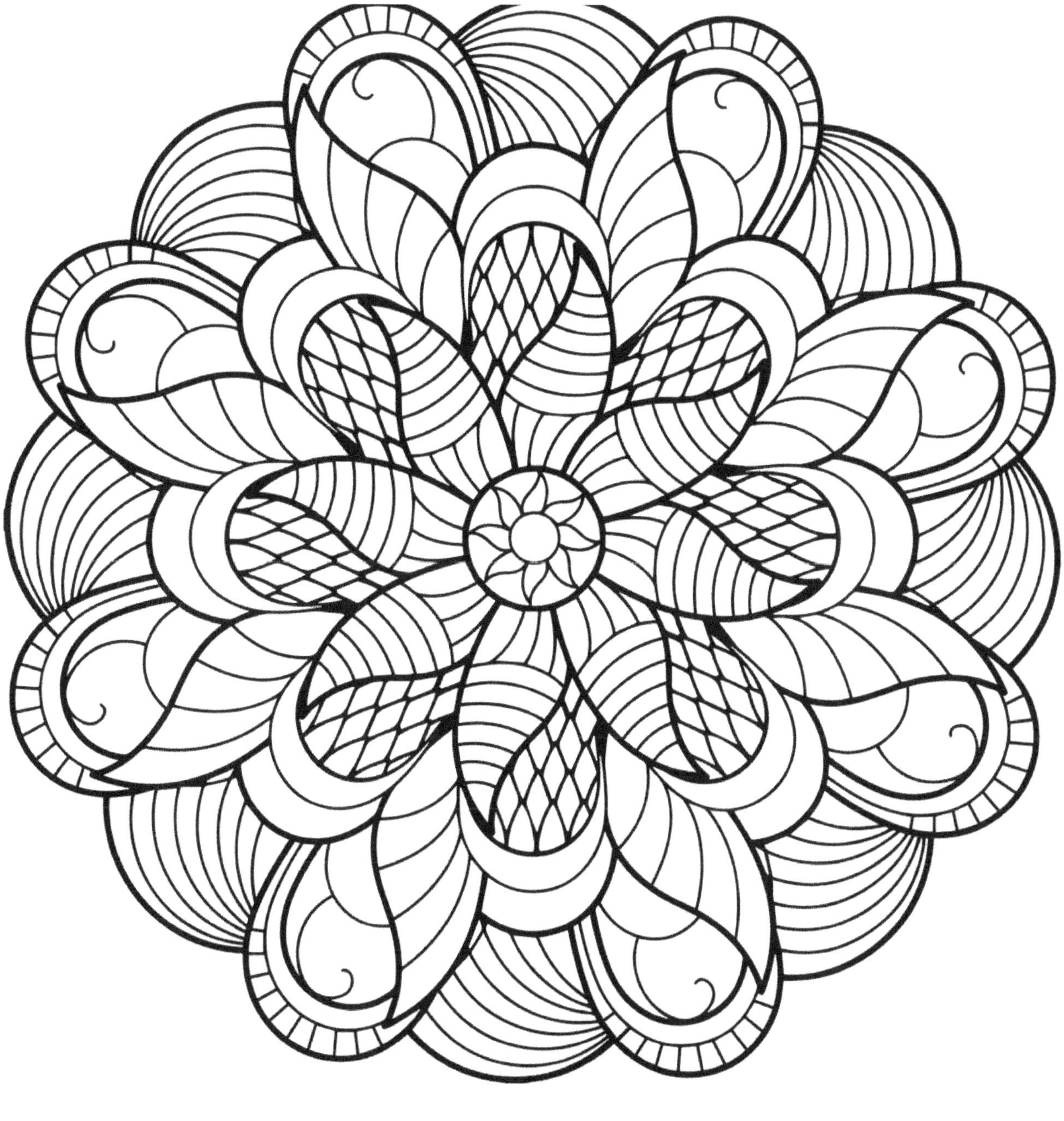

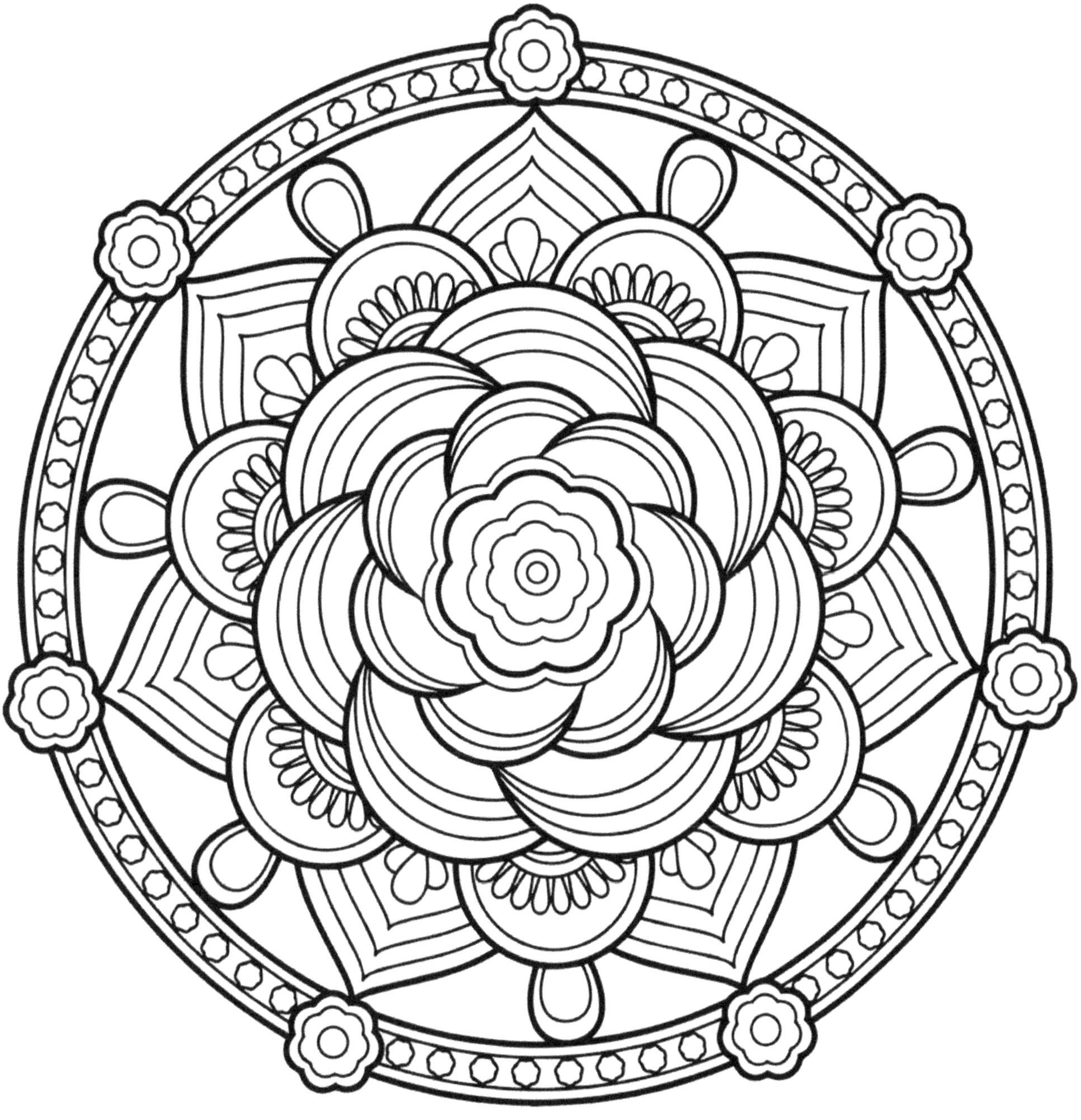

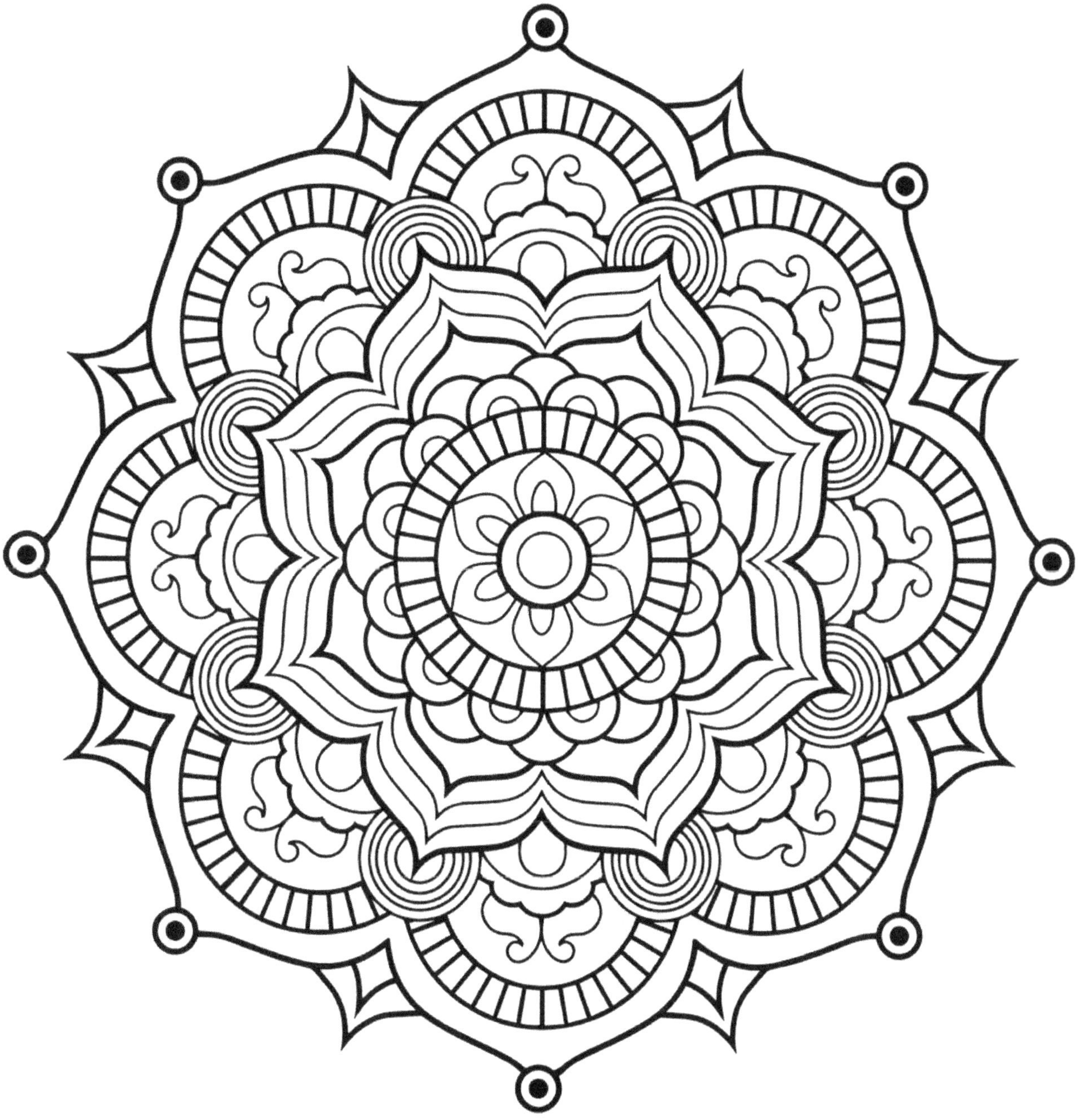

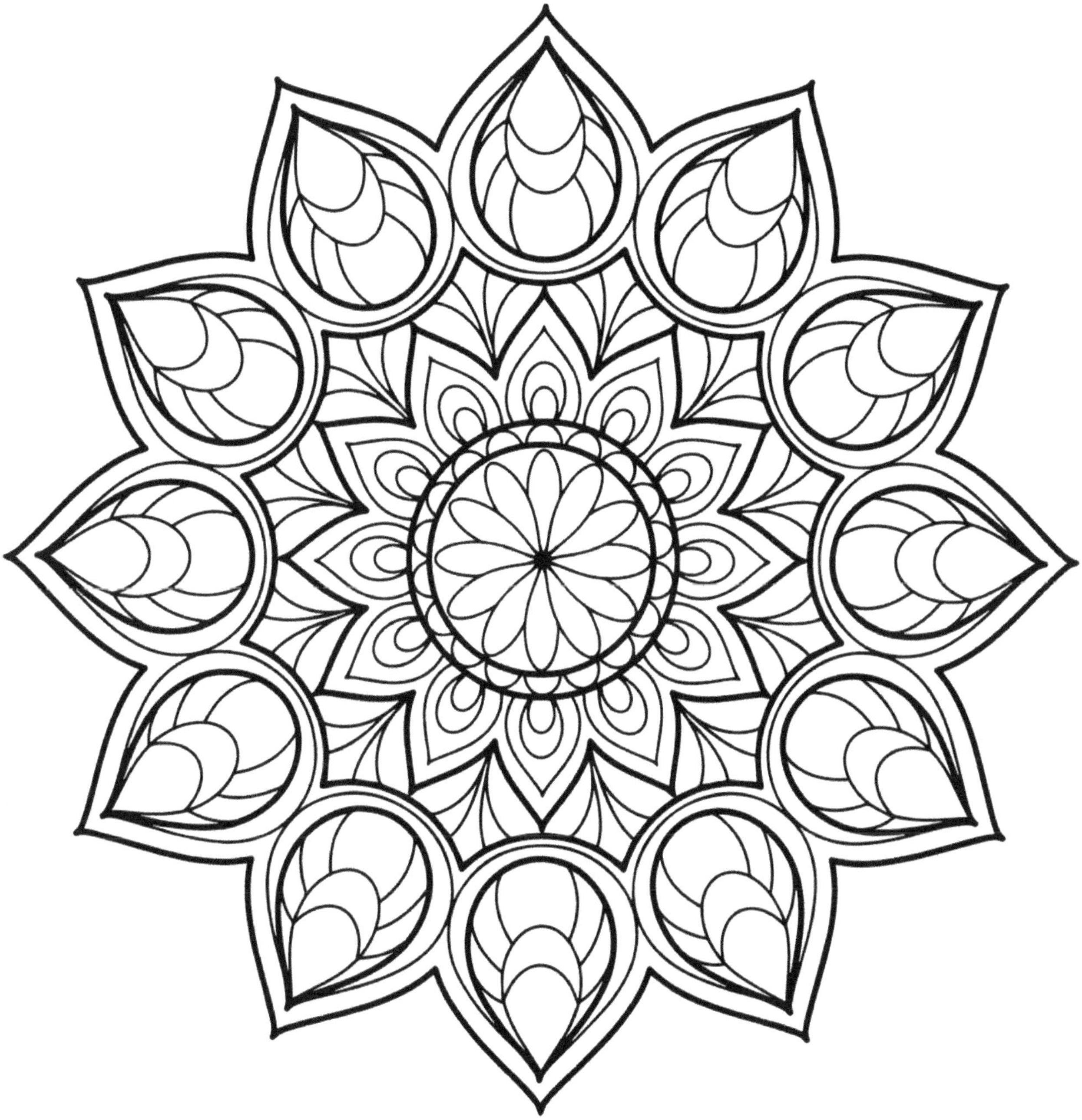

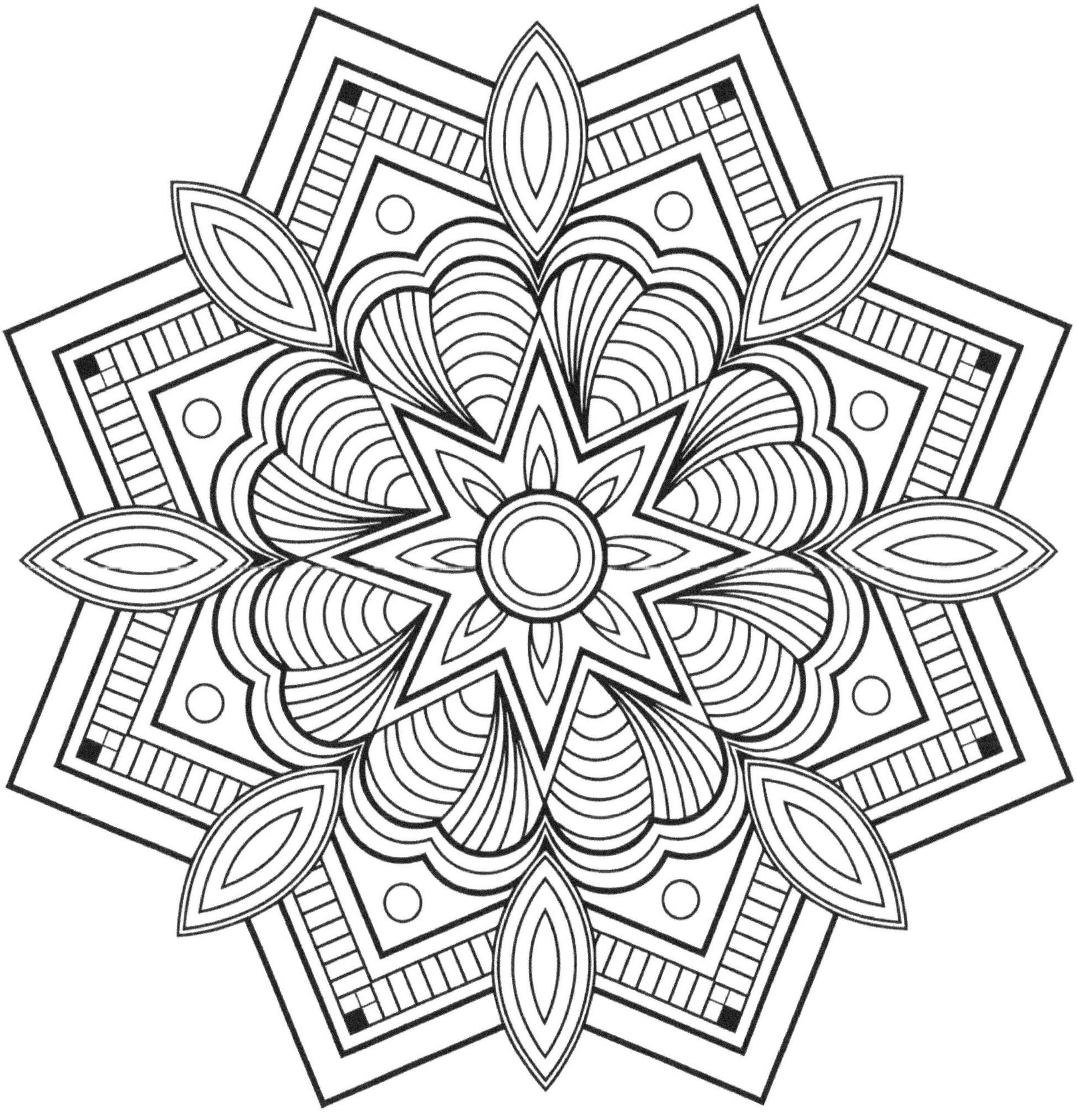

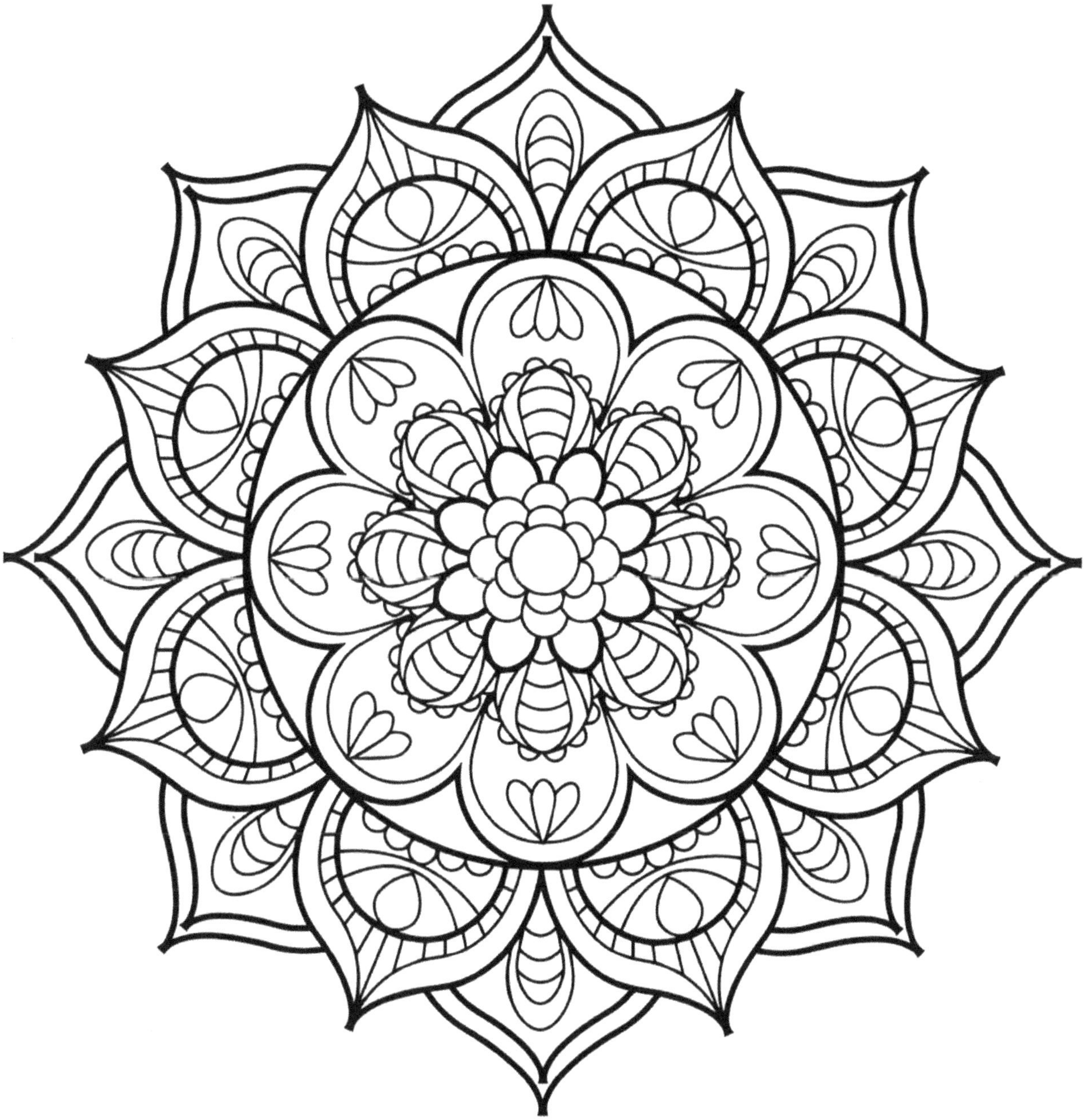

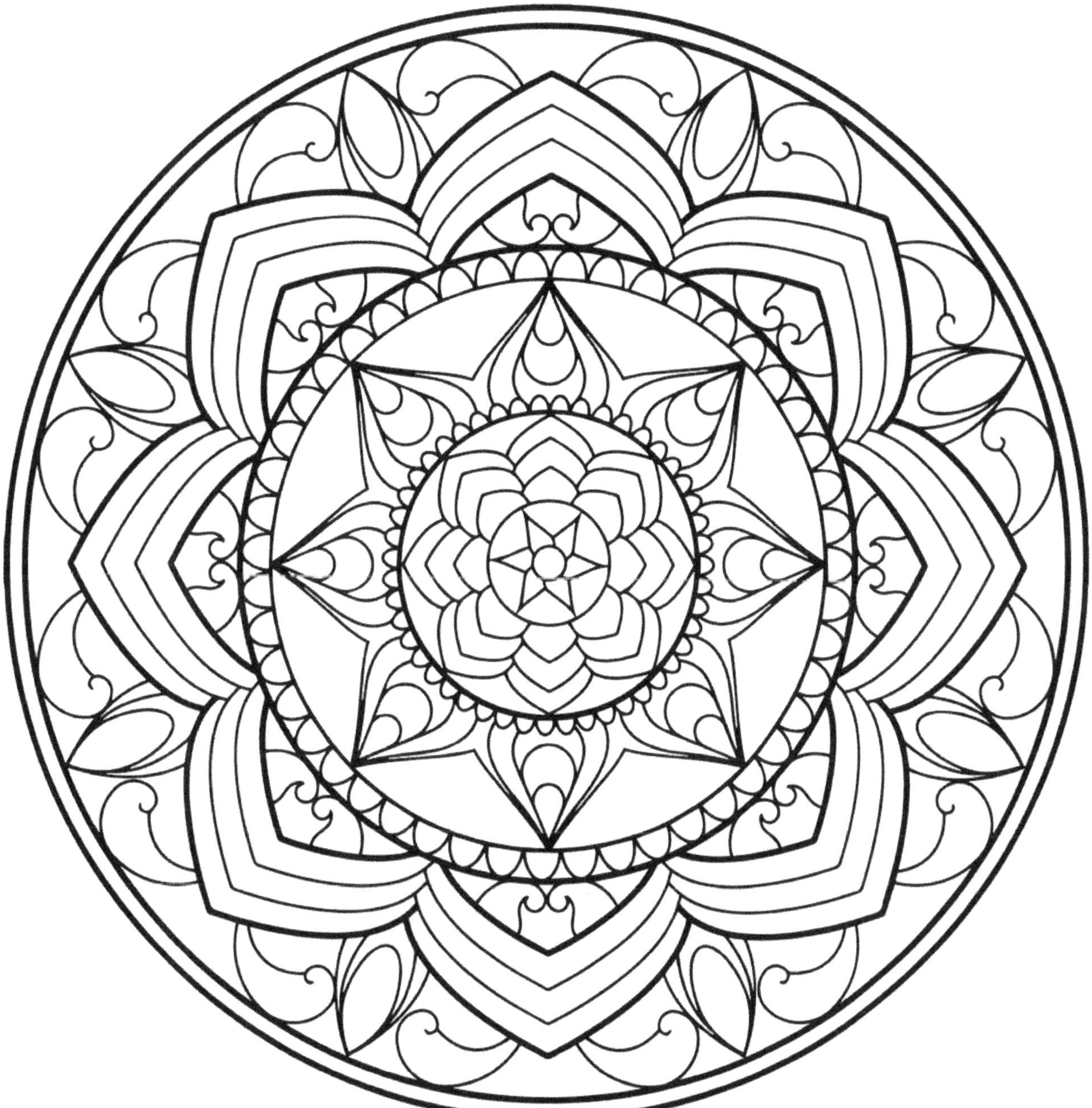

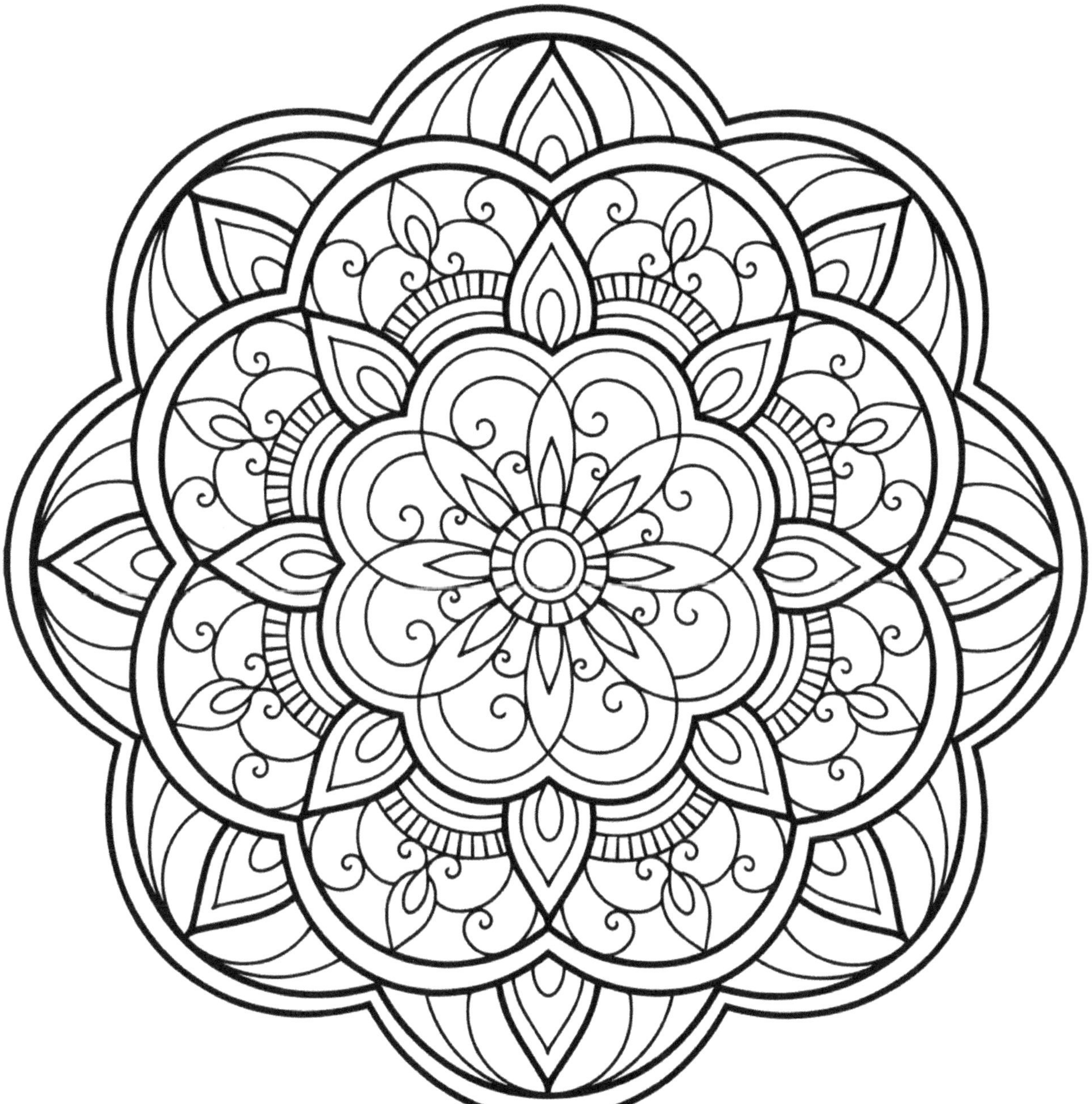

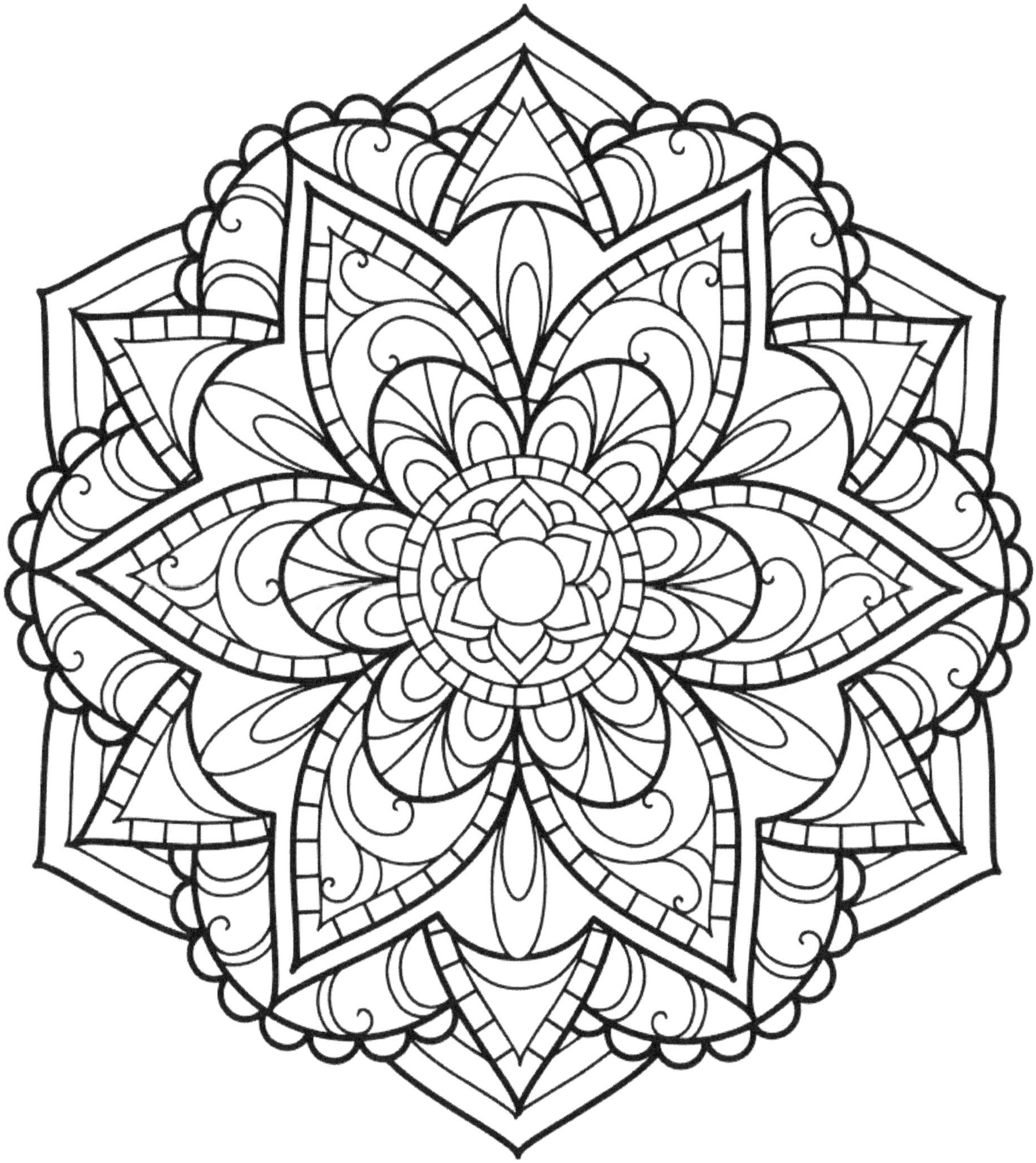

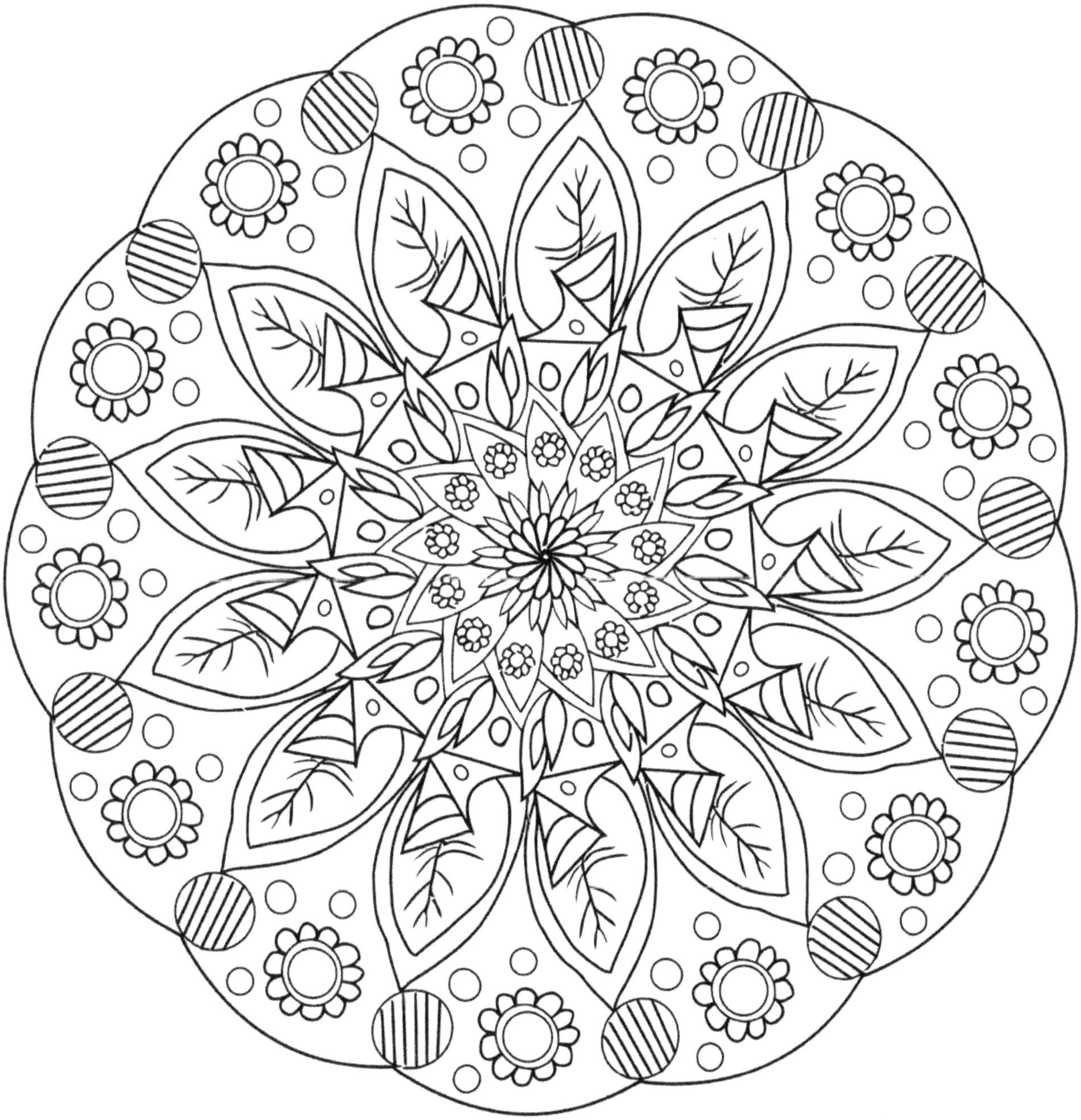

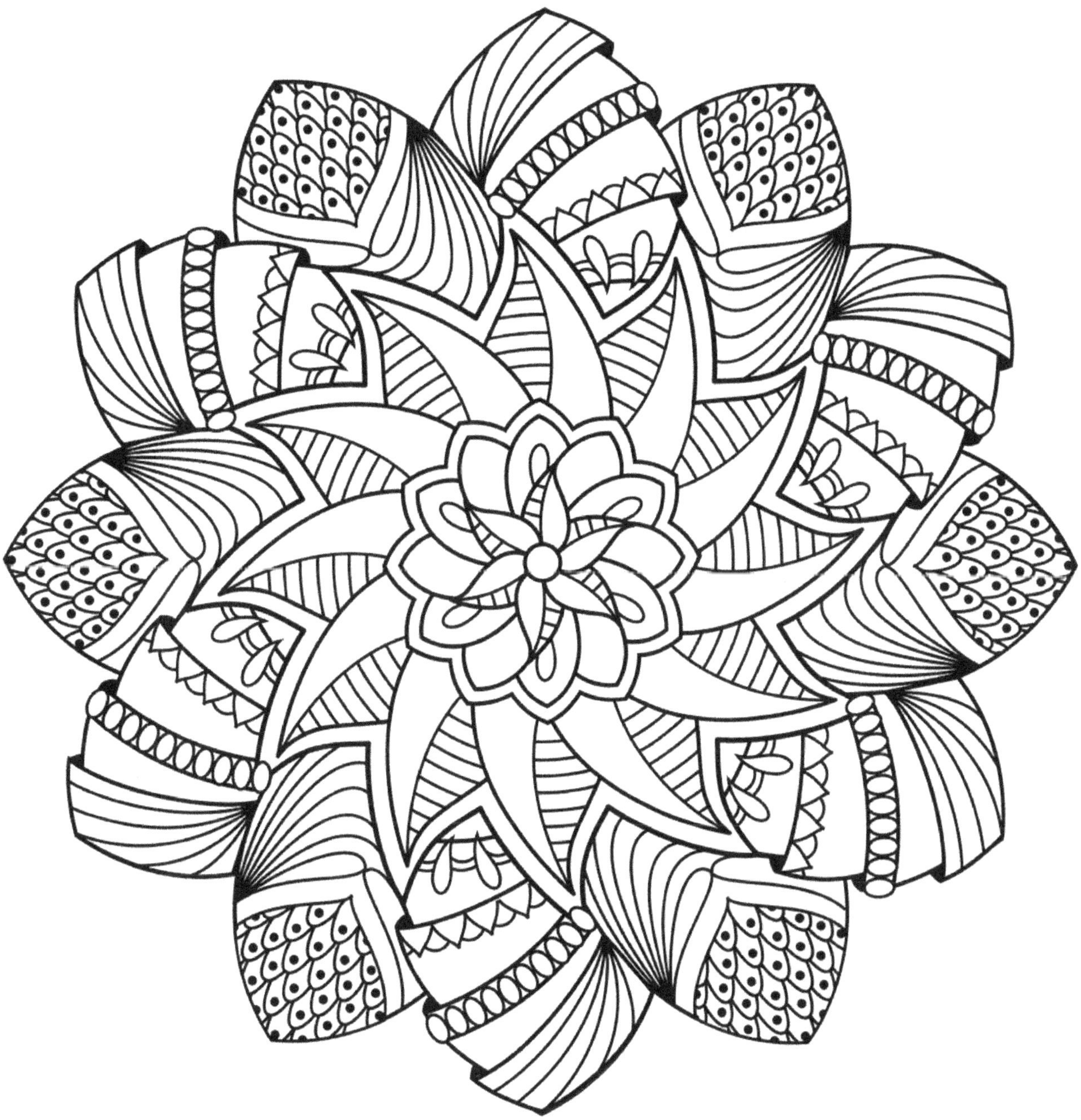

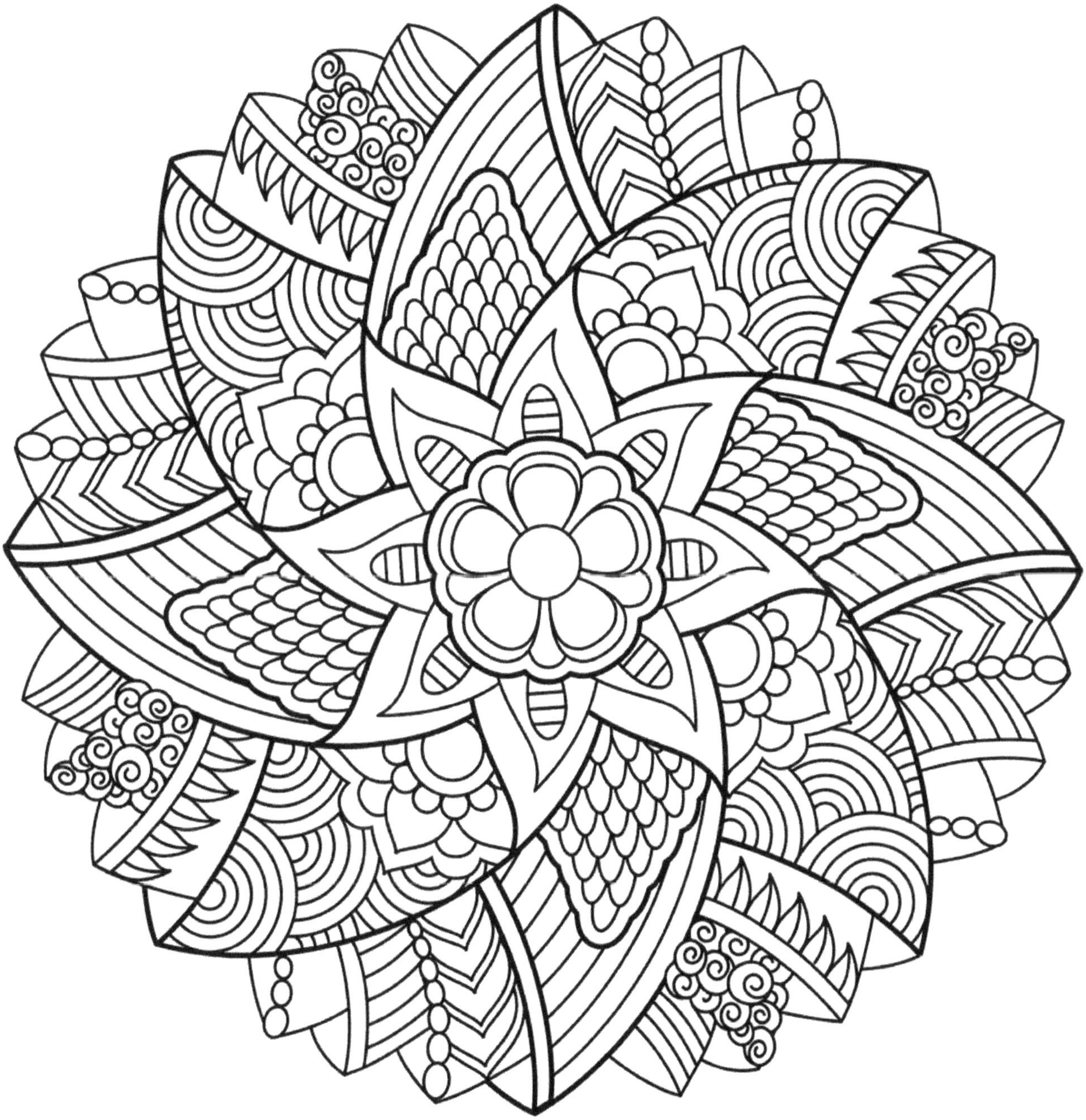

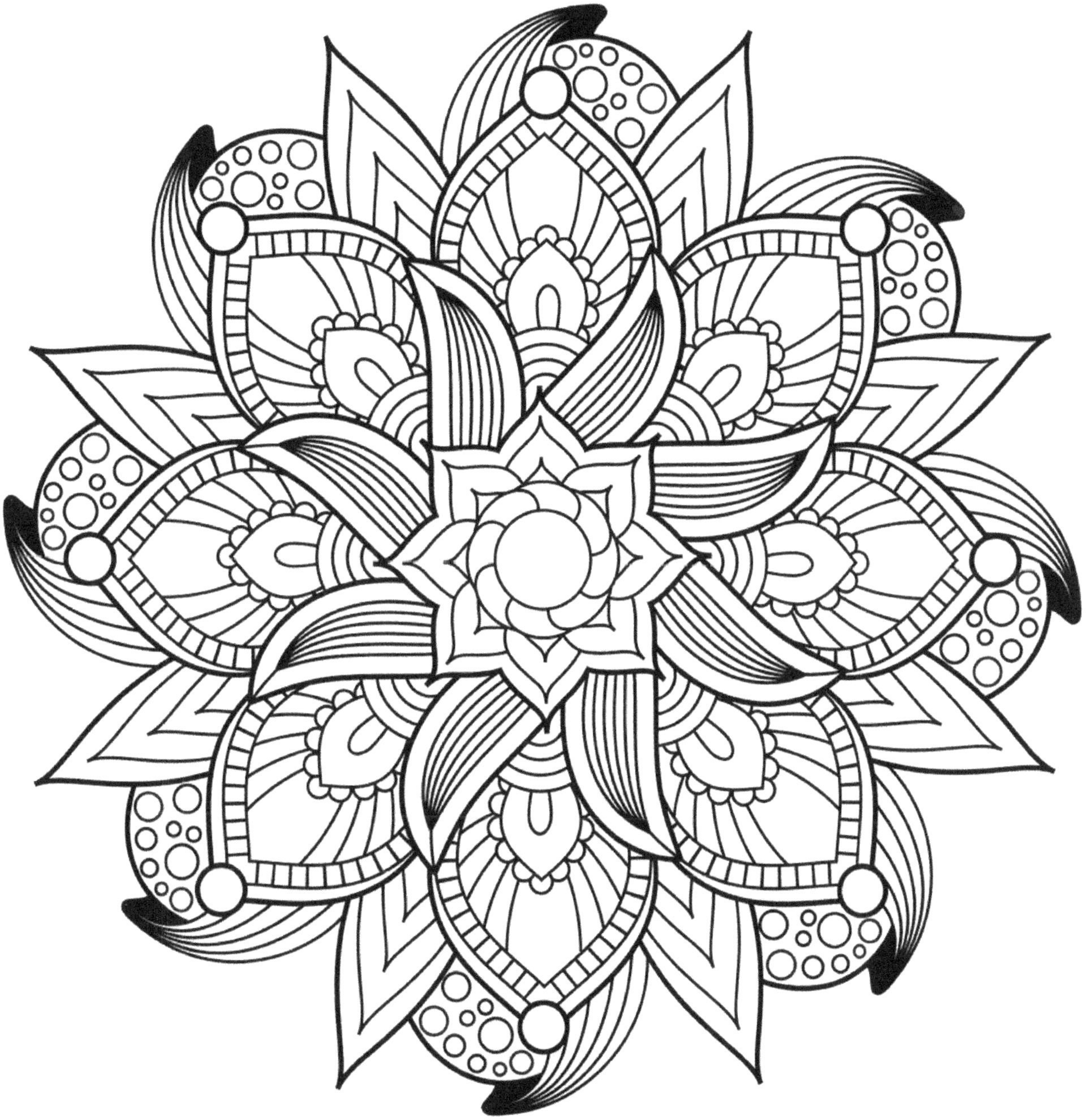

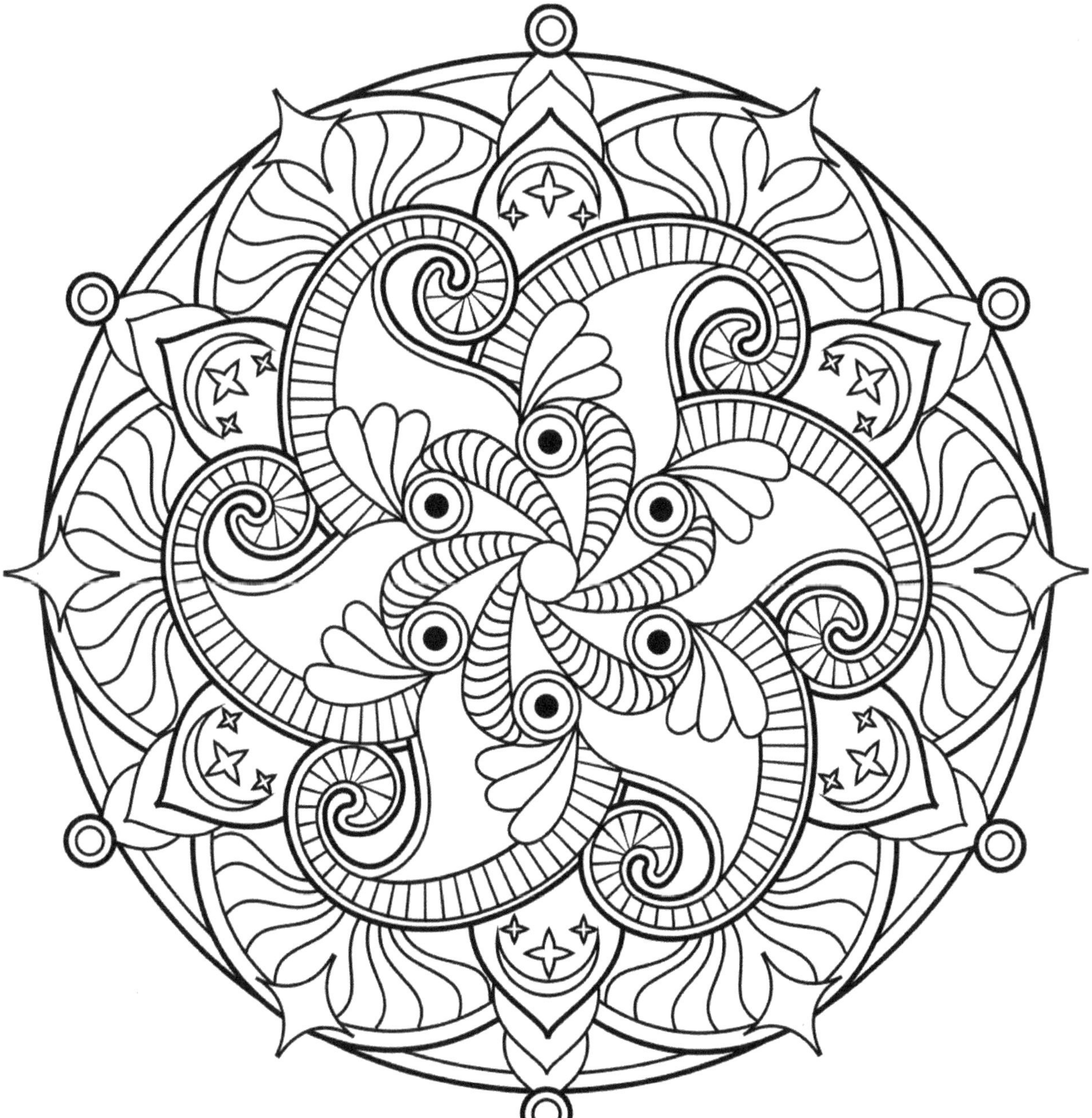

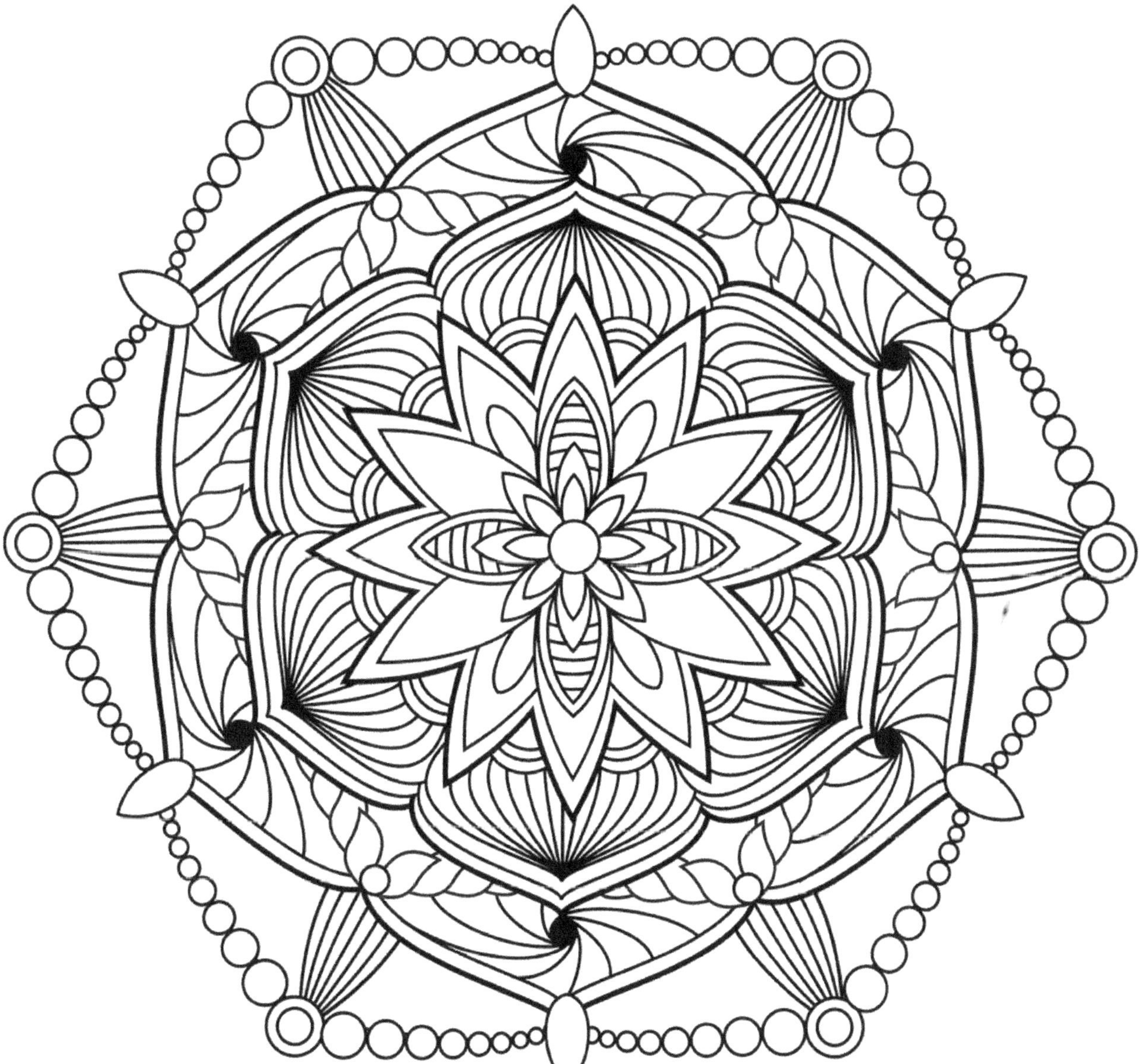

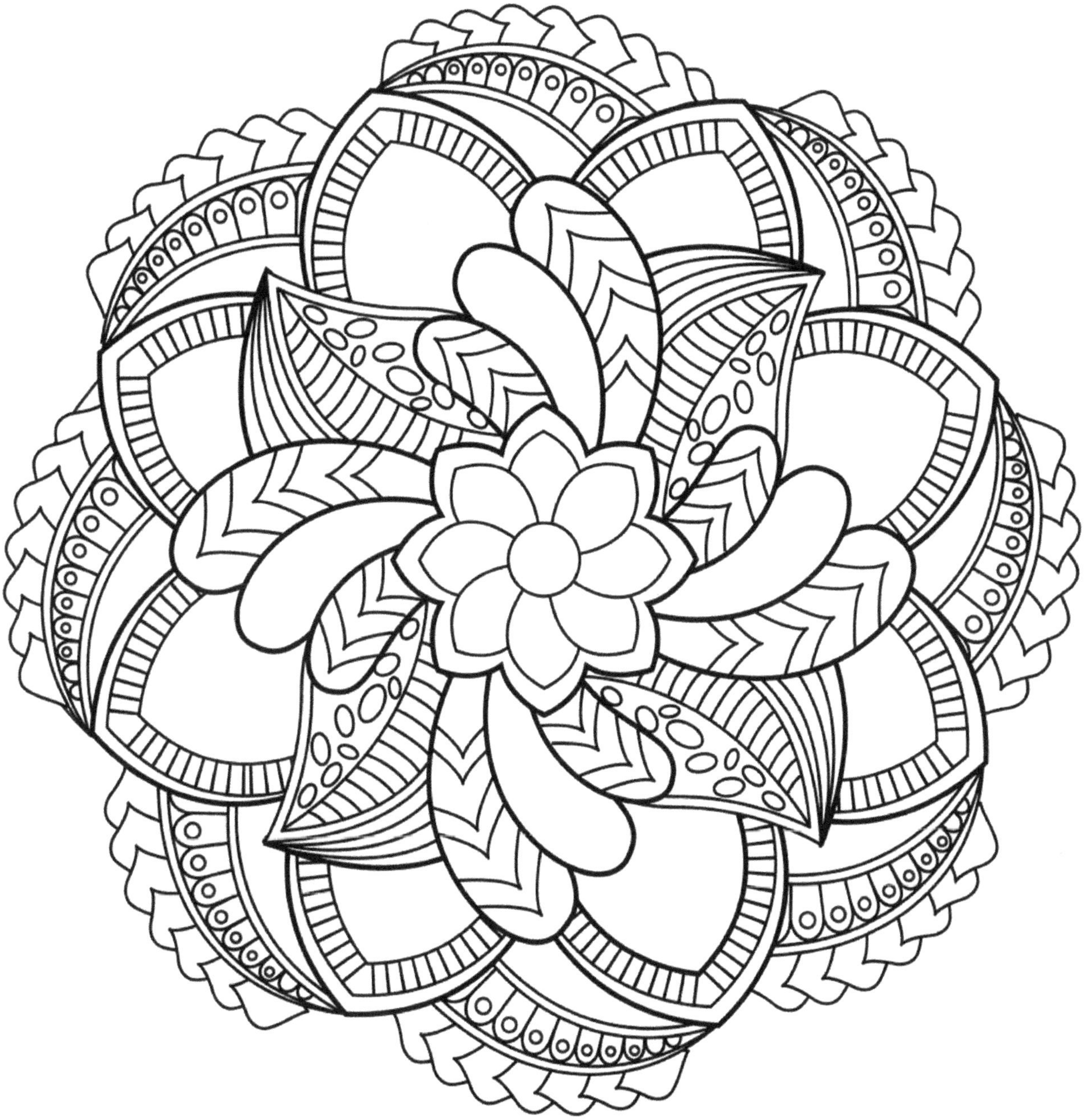

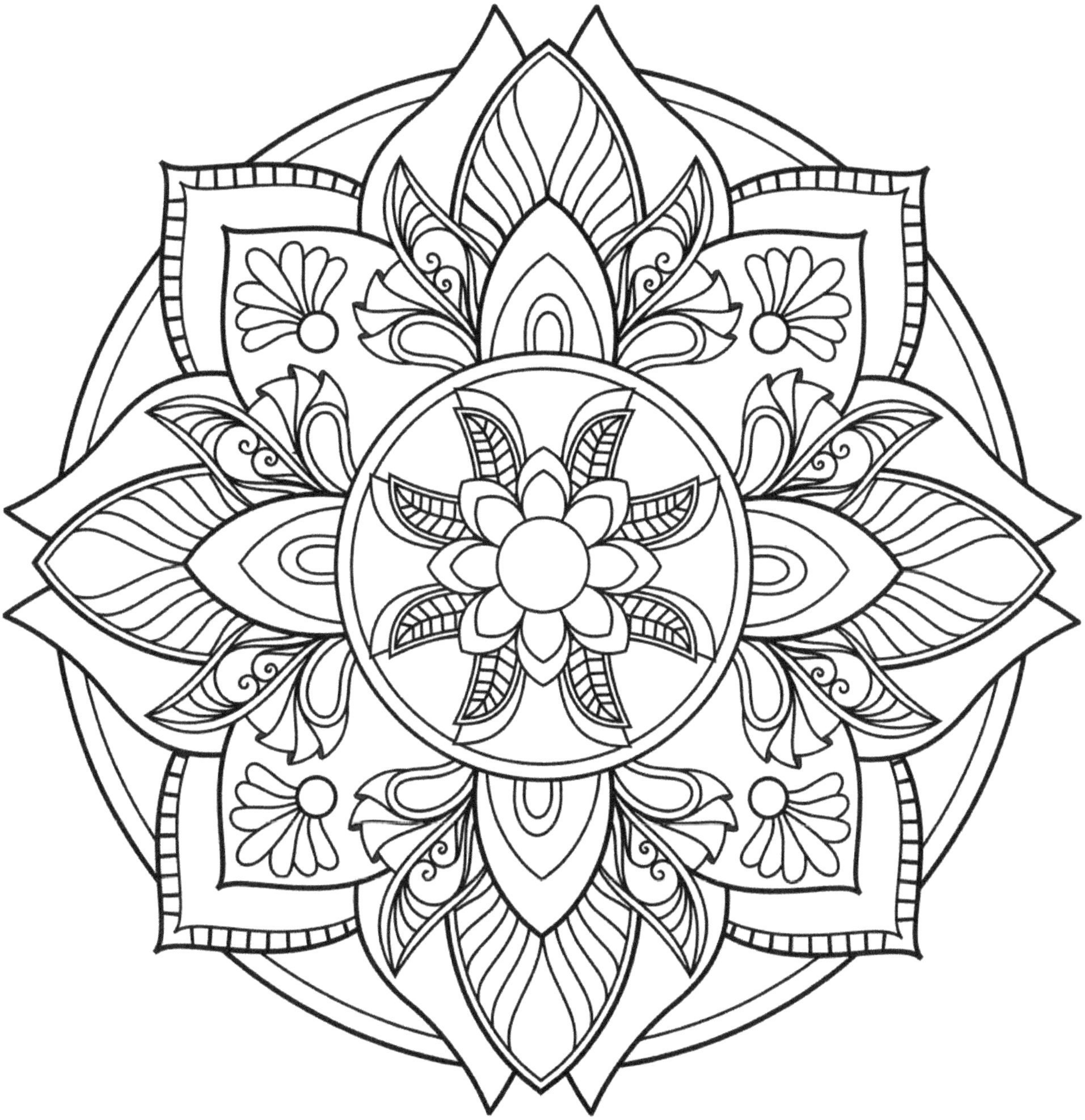

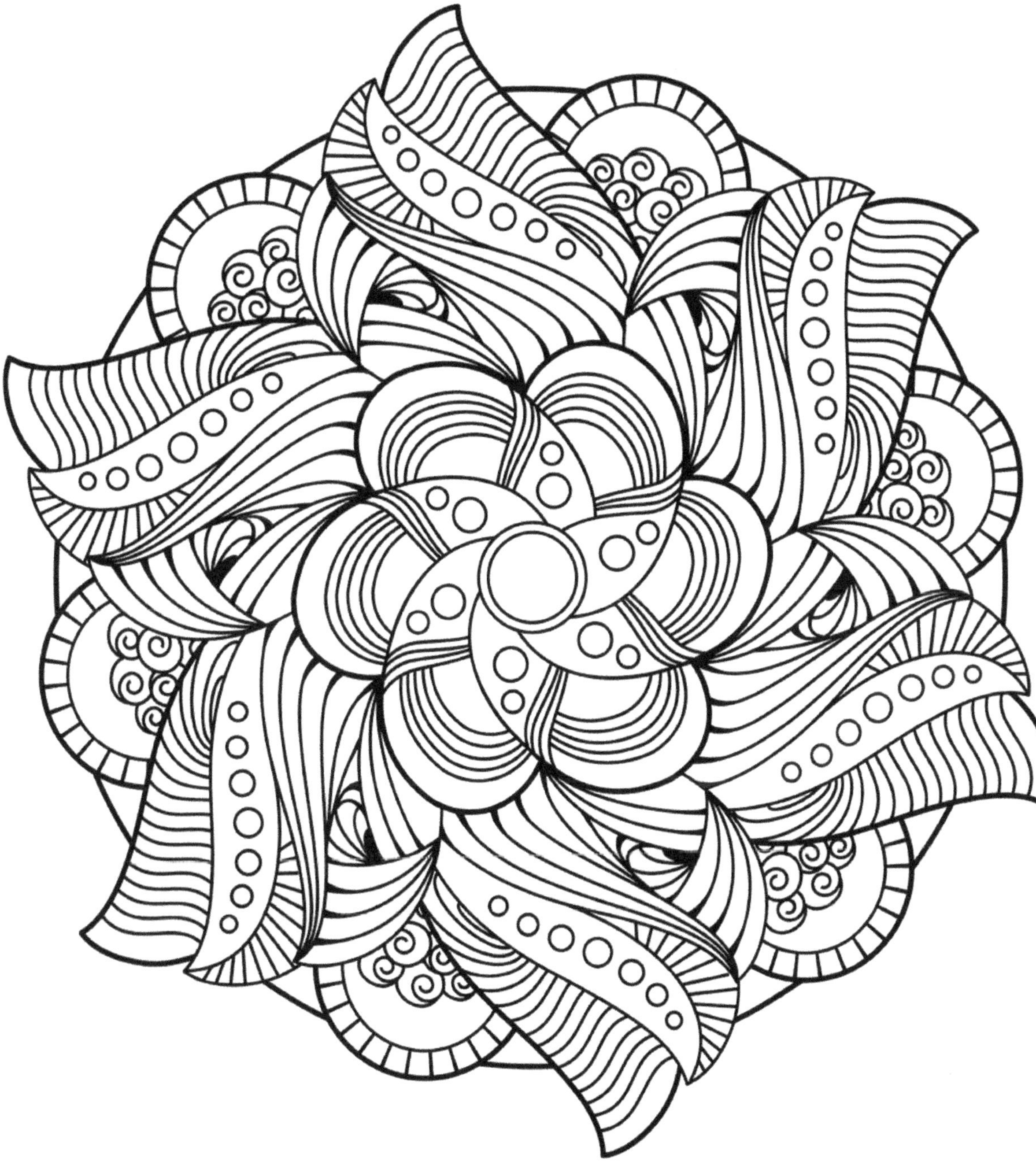

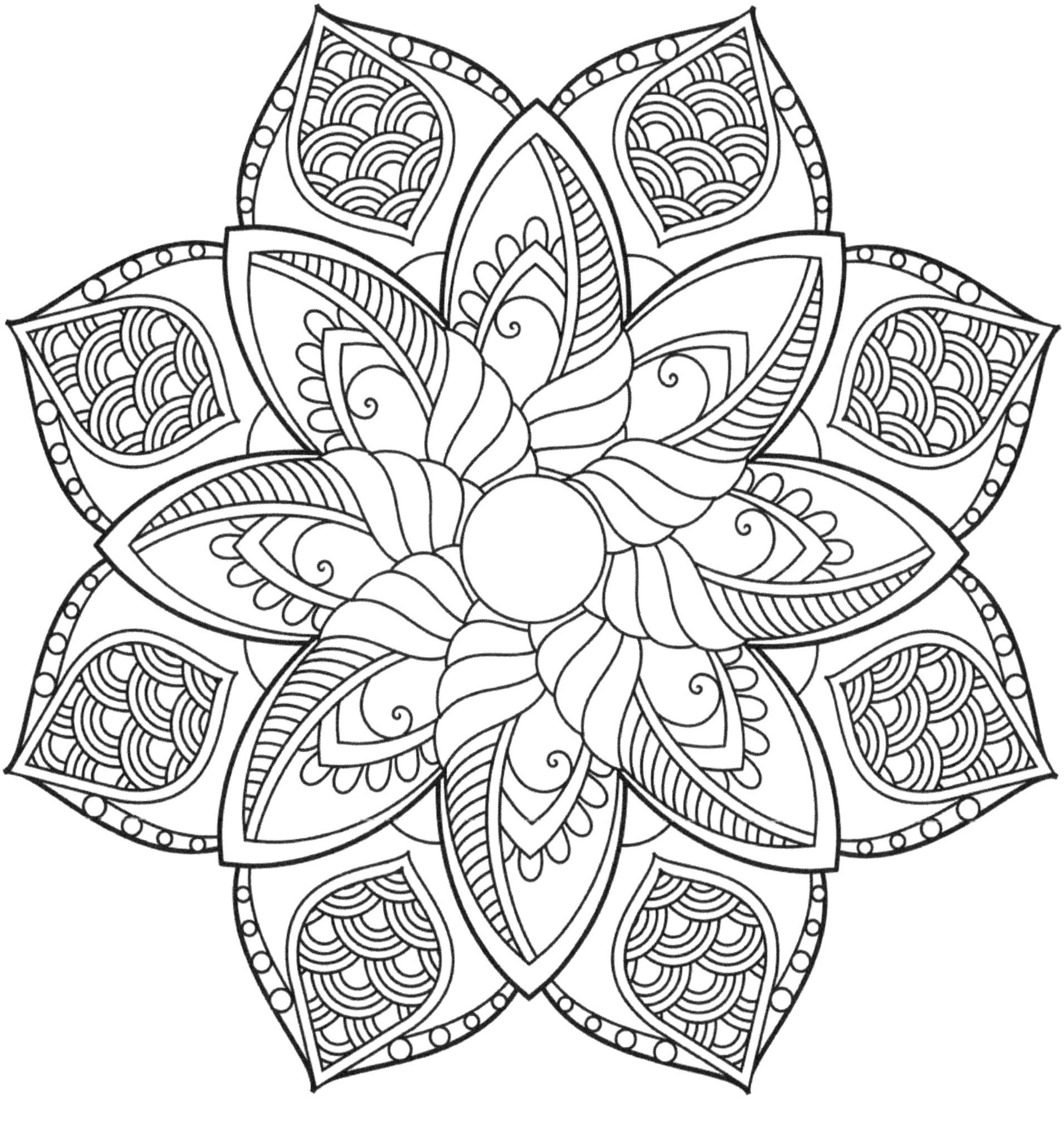

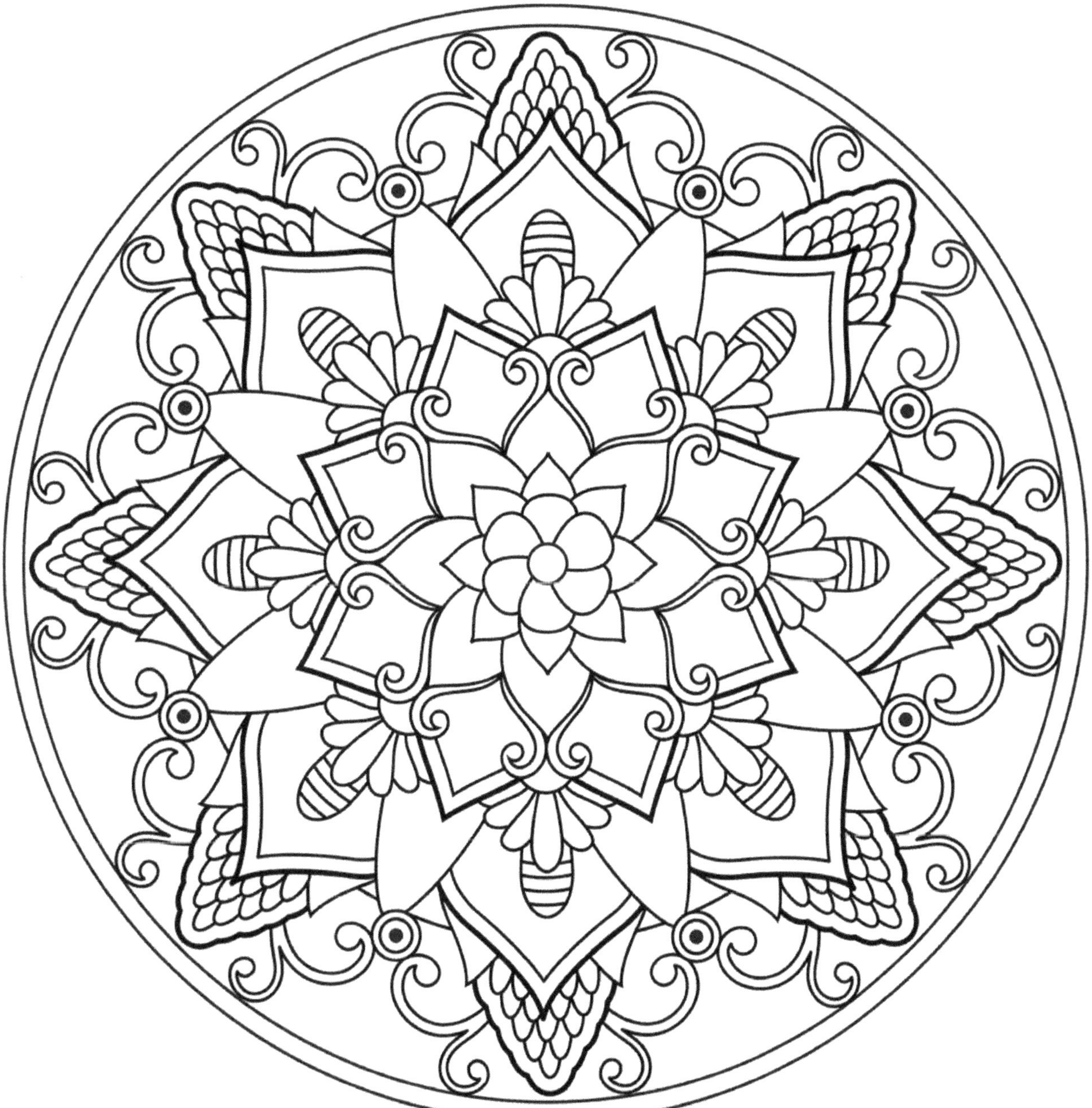

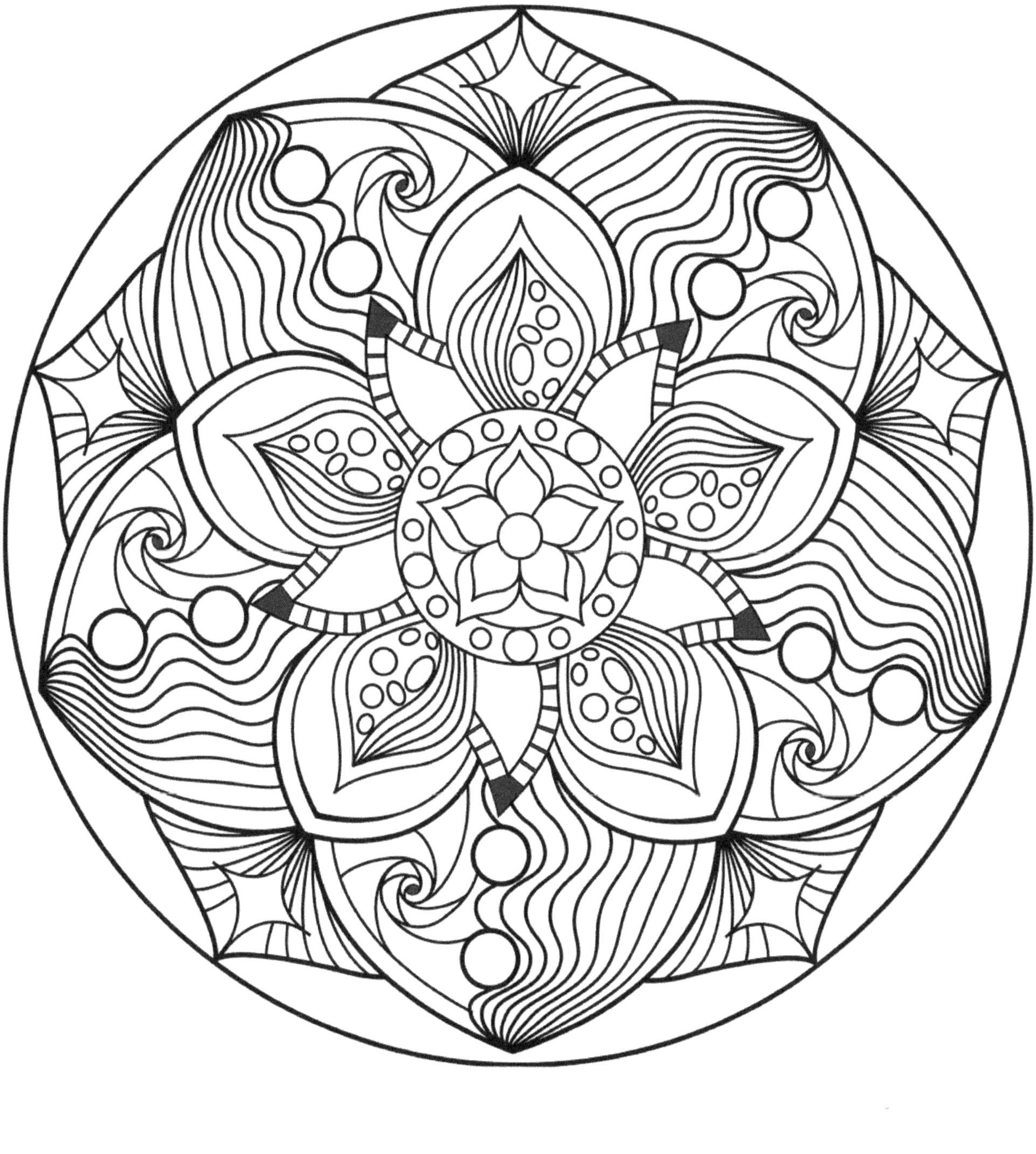

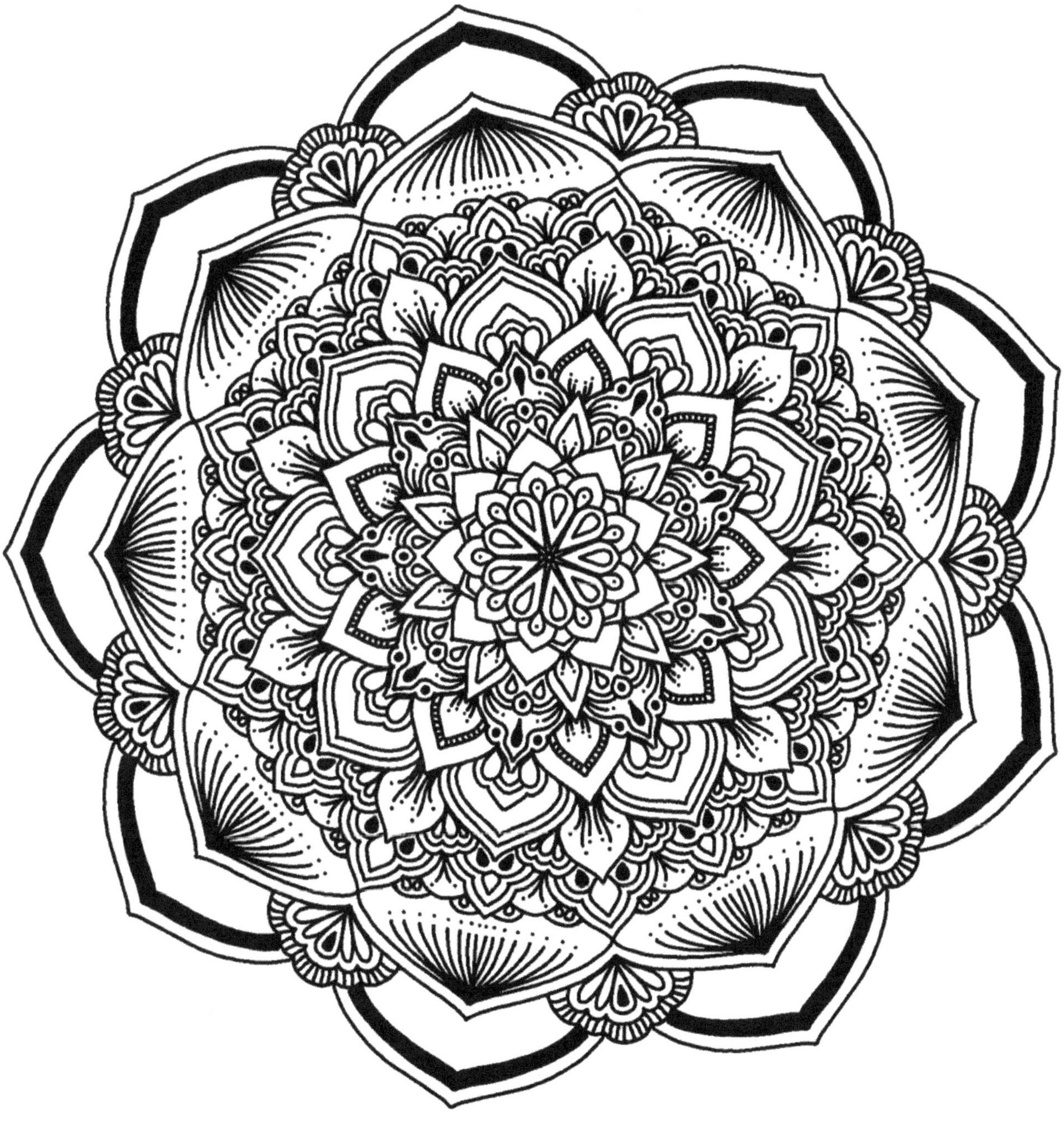

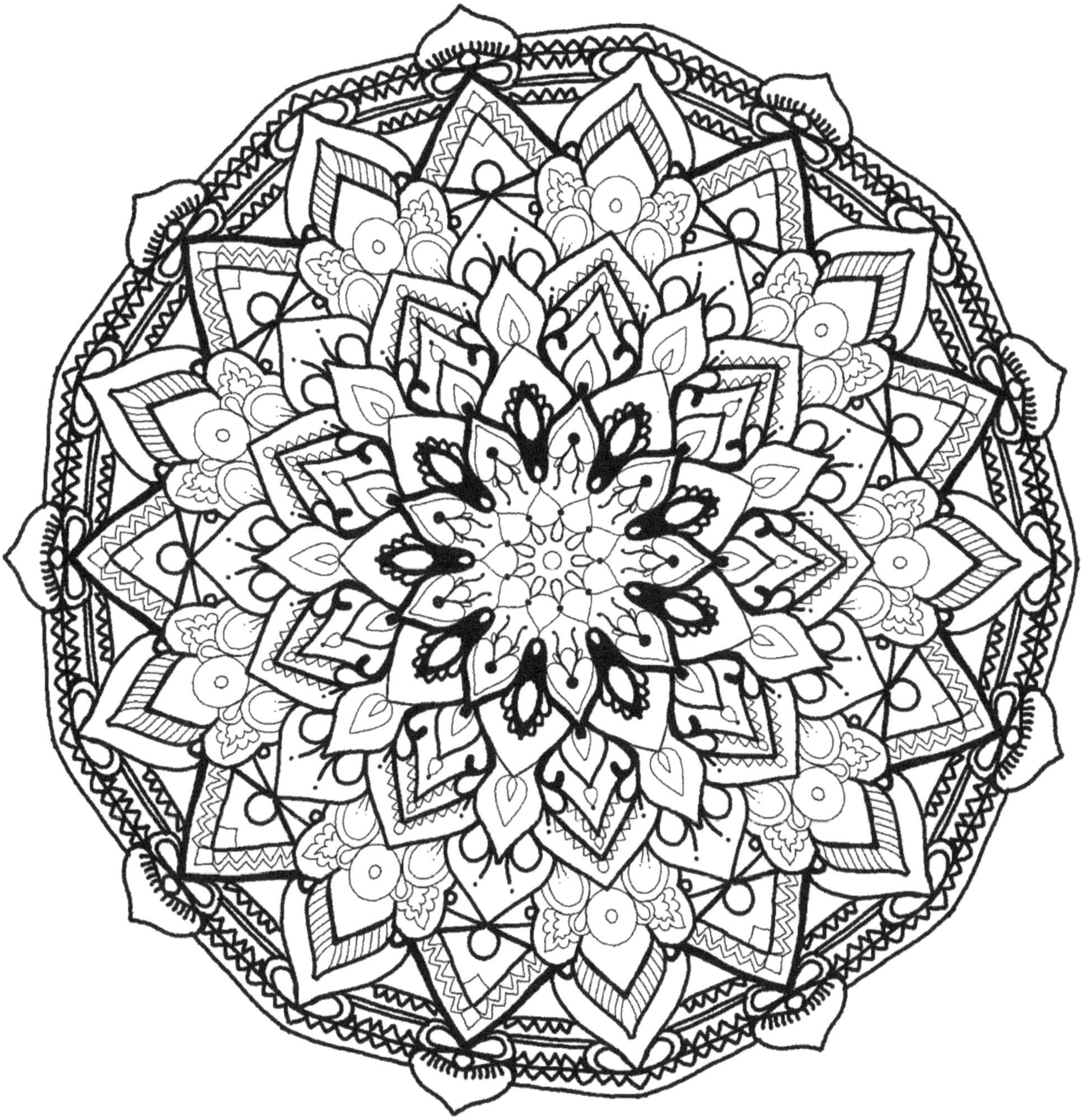

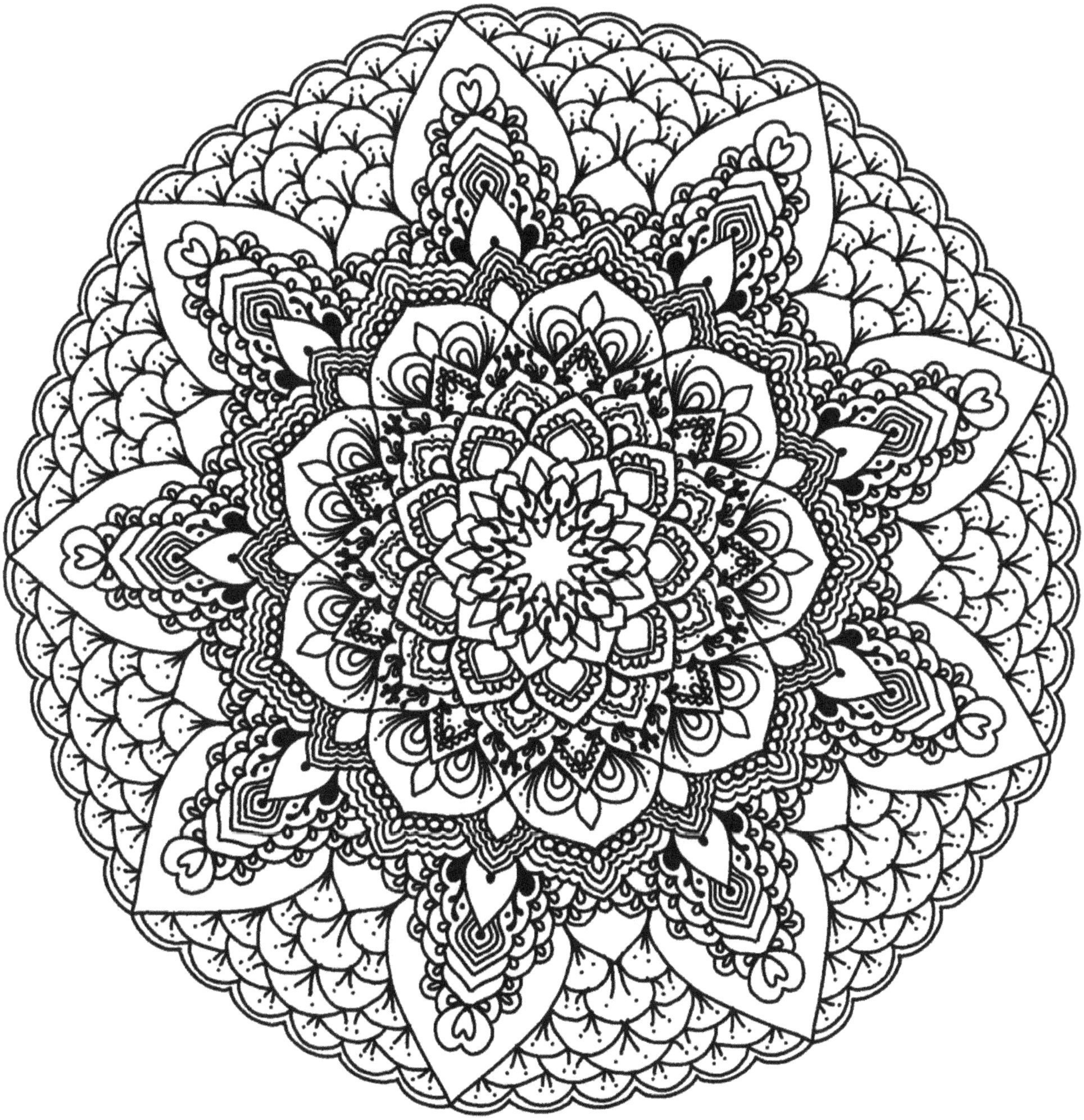

www.ingramcontent.com/pod-product-compliance
Lightning Source LLC
Chambersburg PA
CBHW080557060326
40689CB00021B/4885
9781096625353